WEAR YOUR **WARRIOR**

First published in 2021 by Dean Publishing
PO Box 119
Mt. Macedon, Victoria, 3441
Australia
deanpublishing.com

Copyright © Katrina Wurm

All rights reserved. No part of this publication may be reproduced, stored in a retrieval system or transmitted in any way or by any means, electronic, mechanical, photocopying, recording or otherwise, without the prior written permission of the publisher.

Cataloguing-in-Publication Data
National Library of Australia
Title: Wear Your Warrior: The Evolution of the Stress-Free Super Mum
Edition: 1st edn
ISBN: 978-1-925452-37-2
Category: Memoir/self-help

This is an autobiography, the author has tried to recreate events, locales and conversations from her memories of them. In order to maintain anonymity of certain individuals in some instances names, occupations and places have been changed to protect individuals. Certain identifying characteristics and details such as physical properties, occupations and places of residence may have changed.

This book is a personal memoir and not intended as a substitute for the medical advice of physicians. The reader should regularly consult a physician in matters relating to his/her health and particularly with respect to any symptoms that may require diagnosis or medical attention. This is not intended for medical purposes or promote any particular type of treatment than that recommended to the individual from their own medical team- each person is different.

The views and opinions expressed in this book are those of the authors and do not necessarily reflect the official policy or position of any other agency, publisher, organisation, medical team, employer or company. Assumptions made in the analysis are not reflective of the position of any entity other than the author(s) – and, these views are always subject to change, revision, and rethinking at any time.

The authors or organisations are not to be held responsible for misuse, reuse, recycled and cited and/or uncited copies of content within this book by others.

WEAR YOUR **WARRIOR**

The Evolution of the Stress-Free

KATRINA WURM

Contents

Chapter 1 — 9
Introduction to Wear Your Warrior

Chapter 2 — 19
Self-Love: Selfish or Selfless?

Chapter 3 — 37
Control

Chapter 4 — 55
Buy Back your Time

Chapter 5 — 73
Planning

Chapter 6 — 95
Your Dream Day

Chapter 7 — 109
Have You Kondoed?

Chapter 8 — 121
The Law of Attraction and all that *frou-frou*

Chapter 9 — 135
Welcome to Motherhood

Chapter 10 — 153
Passion Project

Chapter 11 — 161
Summary of Tools, Techniques and Quotes from Each Chapter

Testimonials/Case Studies/Working with Clients — 181

Appendices — 189

About the Author — 197

Acknowledgements — 202

Endnotes — 205

Permissions — 206

Dedication

To my boys, Michael, Andreas and Anton, you are my WHY.
Love you around the world and back again,
to the moon and back again,
and to infinity and beyond.

'You only live once,
but if you do it right,
once is enough.'

Mae West

CHAPTER 1

Introduction to Wear Your Warrior

*W**ear Your Warrior.* What does that mean, and why does it relate to me and my life?

Merriam Webster defines a warrior as, 'a person engaged or experienced in warfare *broadly*: a person engaged in some struggle or conflict'[1]; whereas the Cambridge Dictionary defines a warrior as, 'a soldier, usually one who has both experience and skill in fighting, especially in the past'.[2]

If we look to the past and focus on female warriors throughout history, there are many examples of true strong female fighting warriors, whether they were defending their land, their faith, their ruler or their ideals.

When I think of female warriors, the first to come to mind is Joan of Arc. Her influence ended the siege of Orleans in nine days, and at 17 years old, she played a key role in commanding France's Army. Her forte was strategy over senseless slaughter. Many monuments celebrating her life and achievements exist around the world. My favourite would have to be the gold statue near the Louvre and Tuileries Gardens, in the Place des Pyramides in Paris.

Queen Boudicca is another favourite. In a heavily male-dominated society, with 100,000 at her command, she toppled the Roman capital of Britain, Camulodunum. She went on to destroy cities, and her victories forced the Emperor Nero to consider pulling out of Britain completely. An impressive monument to her stands on the western side of Westminster Bridge.

An elusive female Samurai also makes my list. Nakano Takeko was educated in literacy and martial arts before becoming a distinguished warrior in the Boshin War (1868-1869). During the annual Aizu Autumn Festival, young girls today take part in a procession commemorating her actions. Her monument is by the Hokaiji Temple near Fukushima.

Finally, my favourite has to be the fictional Wonder Woman, Diana. Wonder Woman is the daughter of Queen

Hippolyta, the leader of the Amazons who live on the island of Themyscira. We all know the story of how she came to America to fight injustice and became a hero to every little girl. I so wanted her invisible jet – oh, and the Lasso of Truth. Who wouldn't want that?

To research more inspiring female warriors from history, have a look at the Rejected Princesses website at www.rejectedprincesses.com. I totally recommend it.

CURVEBALLS AND DWARF PLANET PLUTO

At stages throughout my life, many people have said to me, 'You need to write a book. No one would believe your life!' Am I that unusual, that special?

Trust me, I am not special, and neither are you. We all have the same stuff going on. We all get hit by curveballs. Some of us get hit by a curveball the size of an actual baseball; some of us get hit by a curveball the size of the planet Pluto (oops, sorry, 'dwarf' planet Pluto. My son would not have let that mistake slide – more on him, later).

Most of my curveballs have been of the dwarf planet Pluto size. You know, if I had my time over or had a choice to choose my curveballs or someone else's, I would probably choose mine.

This book is for you if you have been thrown a curveball that has altered your course, or if you woke up one morning and thought, 'How the hell did this become my life? This is certainly not what I was dreaming of back in my bedroom listening to Aerosmith, Duran Duran, Bon Jovi, U2, AC/DC, Wham, Take That or ... (insert band here depending on your musical tastes and generation!).

This book is also for you if you feel you have lost yourself somewhere. Was it living for someone else, your parents perhaps (I can so relate to that), your children, maybe even your partner? Are you feeling weighed down, overwhelmed, and under pressure to be perfect, to be it all and do it all?

For over 40 years, I have found that there are timeless solutions that never fail me. Nothing in this book is new; it may have a new slant on it or a new perspective. But the tools and techniques I use in my life, and now have the privilege and honour of coaching others on, work with one major disclaimer. You have to implement them. Lying on the couch in your pyjamas, drinking a mojito, waiting for your life to change. Sorry, sunshine – that's not going to happen, no matter which universe you live in.

I would love to give you the magic pill, the 'buy my program and get rich, organised and healthy in seven days' sell. But guess what? If you want to make a change in your life, some work has to be done, and it all starts NOW, WITH YOU!

My life certainly wasn't going to look like this. I was dreaming of law, or maybe journalism. I was into protesting about nuclear disarmament, child slavery and hunger. I had a strong internal hunger to fight against oppression and injustice. Organising a school-wide oval sit-in probably didn't help my chances of being considered school captain material at the time.

Yet here I am, a survivor, a warrior. Every time a curveball came my way, I took the hit, felt the impact and let the bruise develop. I got back up and said to the world, 'Okay, what's next? Try your best because I am going to keep getting up whatever you throw at me.'

And I did, time and time again. And that is what I want for you – to see that life is surely a gift that many are denied. And by life, I mean living, not just existing, not just getting up and going through the same inane motions day after day. I mean living with every fibre of your being, so that when your feet hit the floor as you get out of bed, the world thinks to itself, get ready, she is up. That is truly living by design and not by default.

I didn't become that lawyer or that journalist.

I did become a strong powerful leader, a person with a story of adversity and pain, disappointments and setbacks, which led me to be the kickass warrior I am today.

The Hero's Journey (Joseph Campbell, 1949)[3] is something you might have come across. It is the theme for most books, movies and parables and is used a lot in personal development. The hero has a call to adventure, meets someone significant, comes up against a challenge, has a revelation, an epiphany, is transformed, atones, and returns to live happily ever after. Think Luke from *Star Wars*, Bilbo Baggins from *The Hobbit* or more recently Star-Lord from *Guardians of the Galaxy*.

Most coaches end up coaching due to an epiphany.

Something happens, and they are called to serve others on the same path. My epiphany was my coach calling me out for not sharing my story and for playing small. I didn't know anything about coaching. I was safe, comfortable, and relatively happy in my middle-class environment, working for a global legacy airline. Yet, something was missing. Don't get me wrong, I loved my job, especially the facilitation and training role that I had. But did it light me up from the inside? No.

Along the way, I was also dealing with those multiple dwarf planet Pluto curveballs as well. And I did have moments of 'why me?' and 'enough already'. If one more person had said to me, *when God closes a door, he opens a window*, they were going to get the full force of the less than pleasant vocabulary picked up from a drill sergeant while on a parade ground!

So, I started a journey that has brought me to this point. It is a journey of reflection, understanding my path, my beliefs, and my conditioning, a journey of planning my life, of asking my true self, 'What is it that I want from this life? What do I want my life to mean? What legacy do I want to leave?'

TIME TO FIND YOUR 'GO-TO' SHOES

Wear your Warrior came from a tool that my coaching mentor, Scott Harris, taught me. Cynthia Freeman outlines it in her book, *The Power of Done*. The tool is called the Five

Star Formula.[4] It is used to deconstruct a negative state or emotion and equally construct a more resourceful state or emotion. I use it with all my clients.

Using a series of questions and physical actions, we can examine what has been holding people back. More exciting for me is using it to guide people into a more resourceful state that they can feel and experience through their thoughts and emotions, and subsequently use in future actions. We practise it and practise it to the point that they can call on it when needed. Eventually, it becomes part of them, and they become unconsciously competent at whatever state they need in particular circumstances.

Should I explain what I mean by unconsciously competent? When we learn something new, we progress through four stages. I will use the act of learning to drive a car to illustrate. I am going to make an assumption here that you have learnt to drive a car at some point, or at least understand the concept. The four stages are unconsciously incompetent (lack of awareness stage), consciously incompetent (awareness stage), consciously competent (step-by-step stage) and unconsciously competent (skilled stage).

The first step is that we don't know what we don't know. Using our learning to drive a car analogy, we haven't sat behind the driver's wheel yet. The second step is to sit in the driver's seat and realise how much we don't know. We are consciously trying to get all the actions in order, especially if driving a manual. The third step is when we start to get it. Things are falling into place. We are driving and are safe and competent, and we know it. However, it is still a conscious effort. The final stage of becoming unconsciously competent is when we are doing it without conscious effort. For example, we drive to work and have that moment where we cannot remember the journey.

For *Wear Your Warrior*, the five-star process is one method for getting you into a state, whatever that state looks like to you, to achieve that goal, get through a situation or overcome something that is holding you back from stepping into your greatness. It's like putting on your Wonder Woman cape. It feels strange at first, even uncomfortable or painful, like a new pair of shoes. Think about that new pair of shoes for a moment. You buy them; they are gorgeous but so uncomfortable. Maybe we will call them limousine shoes, the ones you wear to get picked up in a limo (I wish) and taken straight to the door of wherever you are going, so you need only walk a few steps in the shoes at most. But you wear them again, then again, then again, and you realise they don't hurt anymore. The leather has softened, and they are actually, dare I say it, comfortable. They are your favourite pair now; your 'go to' shoes.

So, keep reading, stay with me on this journey if you want to claim your life back, stand up for yourself in your own shoes (whether they are stilettos or flip flops – no judgement here). Move forward out of that hole, build a bat big enough to slam those curveballs out of the ballpark and learn to say yes and figure it out later.

'I choose

To live by choice, not by chance,

To be motivated, not manipulated,

To be useful, not used,

To make changes, not excuses,

To excel, not compete.

I choose self-esteem, not self-pity,

I choose to listen to my inner voice,
not to the random opinions of others.

I choose to do the things that you won't so
I can continue to do the things you can't.'

Dr Bohdi Sanders

'You are the
longest commitment
you'll ever have.

You have to make you
a priority.'

Anon

CHAPTER 2

Self-Love: Selfish or Selfless?

Whitney Houston released a song in 1985 called 'Greatest Love of All'. At the time, I didn't know what to make of it. What did she mean? What did learning to love yourself actually mean? I was a teenager at high school navigating a world I didn't understand. Did it mean having the occasional massage, the regular nail or hair appointment, the taking time for myself idea?

I have since discovered the song was written by Michael Masser for *The Greatest*, a 1977 film about the life of boxer Muhammad Ali. Yet the lyrics stayed with me, and the song is one I still listen to on a regular basis.

So, when do we learn to love ourselves, or more accurately, when did we learn not to?

As babies, we know no different; we are just a sum of our parts. Our bodies go where they are placed. We learn to roll, then crawl, then walk, run and dance. Our bodies are a vehicle to move us from one place to the next, whether by walking, dancing or skipping. We are just us, and our self-talk is about our needs and wants.

Then something happens to change things, and our self-talk changes somewhere along the way. We watch, we observe, we listen, we learn. What is the self-talk of our significant people, our caregivers, the adults surrounding us, the ones who are showing us what this world means and how to navigate it?

For some of you, this journey of discovery was positive. It was one of light, love, achievement and confidence, of being able to take on the world and win at everything and anything.

For many, like me and a number of my clients, the journey through childhood wasn't smooth, and the lessons we learnt through observation set us up for negative, destructive consequences later in life.

WALKING ON EGGSHELLS

My childhood started with a broken home. I attribute fault to neither parent. It was the time of the Vietnam War, and many men who went to Vietnam returned not only with physical scars but emotional and mental ones as well. When we were finally able to have the conversation in my twenties, my biological father admitted to the problems he had on returning from Vietnam and the resulting toll on our family.

I do not lay blame on any particular person for what happened at that time. If blame is to be placed at anyone's door, it would be the society of the day and the complete lack of resources and assistance for men returning from a war we did not understand.

My mother took my sister and me away from our father and returned home to her parents. It was like a move out of the frying pan into the fire. Hindsight is a wonderful thing, and I now realise that our grandfather lived his whole life with undiagnosed bipolar disorder (manic depression). He was prone to extreme fits of rage and frustration and occasional violence, often directed at my mother and grandmother. My panic attacks started at a young age.

Then, in 1974, my mum married my stepdad. This was a long, drawn-out process as, even though she had obtained a divorce from my biological father, being a Catholic, she needed an annulment of her first marriage from the Pope to be able to remarry in the eyes of the Church. This was eventually granted. My sister and I gained a stepdad who then legally adopted us, and our surname changed to his.

So, you can imagine the feelings of isolation and difference while attending a small Catholic school. We were children living with our grandparents, and with a divorced mother, who then dared to get remarried, and to top it all off, our surname changed. It was the talk of the community for ages. A couple of years ago, I ran into a classmate from that time, and all she remembered about me was that I was the child whose name changed as it was such a scandal.

We moved into a family home, just the four of us, and started a new life together. Mum fell pregnant, and we welcomed a little brother into the world. His birth was not easy, and Mum needed emergency surgery resulting in a radical hysterectomy. This is when I believe her manic depression really started to surface and affect her day-to-day functioning.

Then came another move, to a new house, a totally new neighbourhood, new school, fresh start, where no one knew our back story.

Our stepdad (who I will refer to as Dad from now on) was working for our grandfather, who not only ruled his home with an iron fist but also the workplace and his employees. Dad was afforded no special treatment as his son-in-law. He worked longer and longer hours. Eventually, he went into local and then federal government.

Mum wasn't coping. Her manic depression was becoming more and more evident. Getting the right blend and type of medication to help her was taking time. Her suicide attempts were becoming more frequent, and her battle with the medication and fluctuating weight became a daily struggle.

So, as a teenager, I learnt that weight was something to be controlled, to obsess over, something by which to judge worth, not only in myself but also in others.

I was having trouble at school as well. I didn't really fit in. I tried so hard to be what I perceived as normal but was living with a big secret at home, a mother whose actions were so far from what I saw in my friend's homes of how a mother should be or behave.

As children, the term 'walking on eggshells' became our daily mantra. We never knew what the day would bring until Mum got out of bed. Some days she didn't get out of bed at all. We learnt not to show emotion, to suppress what we were feeling, any difficulties we were having at school, with teachers, friends or schoolwork. Mum would take any problems of ours as a personal failing, that she had failed us, and a suicide attempt would soon follow.

THE ARMY AND ACHIEVING

My mum is an amazing, brave woman who is living with a mental illness. This was not something she could control, and our home was full of love, laughter and fun on her good days. She could make a boring trip to the supermarket an adventure and would do anything for us. If we had been growing up today, it would have been so different. Today there is so much more support. Mental illness does not have the same stigma society placed on it back in the seventies, eighties and even early nineties. As children, we would have been able to talk openly and freely about our mum's struggles, not keep it behind closed doors. Our dad would have received more support too. He floundered in how to help her and also how to help us.

Being sent away to boarding school saved me. It gave me a chance to breathe, to grow up and take responsibility for just me. It gave me the opportunity to reinvent myself, look at my life and think about which direction I wanted it to take. It was a time of introspection and firm friendships. But that little girl inside me was still seeking approval and, I guess, love from my parents.

So, I achieved, and I achieved, and I achieved. I got into the double degree programme. I was accepted into the ultimate managerial course in Australia, that of army officer training at the Royal Military College, Duntroon. I kept stacking up the degrees, the post-graduate work, Miss Victoria Awards …

Doing the double degree, I excelled at and loved one half; the other was like landing on Mars and speaking an entirely different language! Those of you who know me well get ready to laugh. I was studying banking and finance, two words that today still strike fear in my very heart and soul. I bet my accountant just burst out laughing!

Then the letter arrived that I had been waiting for. I had been accepted into the Royal Military College, Duntroon, in the Australian capital city of Canberra. The selection process had been rigorous, and I had made it. Looking back, it was a decision made to try and gain my dad's approval as a former military officer himself. What a bad decision that was. But you know I never fail. I either succeed, or I learn, and I realised very early on that the Australian Army at that time needed to do some serious work on how it included and treated its female officers.

I returned home, emotionally battered and bruised, to step back into a relationship where we had different views on what a relationship was and what monogamy meant.

My self-esteem and self-worth had been dealt major blows, and I knew that I had to work out a way to look at my life objectively and look for the lessons and the light. Life was still going to test me, and boy did it, but I needed to find a way to be comfortable in my own skin and with my own company because I am the person I spend the most time with.

So, I started implementing strategies, first to learn to like myself and then to love myself. This was certainly not an overnight success. I still struggle today, but now I have methods, routines and practices, to fall back on in those moments of doubt. Would I like to be a rich, successful supermodel? Some days, it would be pretty cool, but at the end of the day, I need to be happy with myself because that's all I've got.

I started another degree. This one was more my style – management and training and development. After that,

I went on to postgraduate work and started working for a global legacy airline.

TRUER THAN TRUE

I genuinely believe that each and every one of us is here for a reason. No one is a mistake, contrary to what someone may have told you. You are all here to make an impact on the world. Whether inventing a cure for a life-threatening disease (would someone hurry up and invent a cure for cancer please!) or being a Mumma bear who gives the best hugs, you are you, and to quote Dr Seuss,

> *'Today you are You, that is truer than true.*
> *There is no one alive who is Youer than You.'*

So how do you learn to love yourself again? How do you learn to look after yourself and practise self-care?

> *'You must take personal responsibility.*
> *You cannot change the circumstances, the seasons,*
> *or the wind, but you can change yourself.'*
> Jim Rohn

THE 100% RESPONSIBILITY PRINCIPLE

The very first step is to take 100% responsibility for your life. If you constantly blame others for your position in life, your current circumstances, your lack of health, wealth or relationships, you need to stop that right now – this minute. You have to give up all the excuses, the victim stories, all the reasons why you can't do something and why you haven't up until now and stop blaming outside circumstances.

The first thing you need to take responsibility for is YOU, yes YOU, and the way you talk to yourself. Yes, I could blame my circumstances, the way I grew up, past relationships, past employers. There are so many people and situations I could easily walk away from and say that it is all their fault. But once you sit down with yourself and your excuses and fairy tales (because that's what they are), you and only you determine how the world is going to treat you and how you are going to show up every day. If you treat yourself as being lesser, you are giving permission to the world to treat you that way as well.

And I am not going to let you.

Let's start taking steps to get back that self-love. We all know women who exhibit healthy self-love. I am not talking about the selfish, narcissist types. We all know people like that. I am talking about the ones who know and accept who they are.

SELF-LOVE SIGNS

People with a healthy self-love exhibit the following signs:

* Confidence

- An ability to say no
- A positive outlook
- An ability to express their needs
- An ability to see their overall strengths and weaknesses and accept them
- An ability to ensure negative experiences do not impact their overall perspective.

Whereas we know we need to do some work if we are exhibiting the following:

- A continual negative outlook
- Low confidence
- An inability to express our needs
- A fear of failure
- A focus on our weaknesses
- Feelings of shame
- A belief that others are better than we are
- Trouble accepting positive feedback.

Do any of these sound familiar? What about the following characteristics?

- Are you extremely critical of yourself?
- Do you downplay or ignore your positive qualities?

* Do you judge yourself and consider yourself to be inferior to your peers?
* Do you use negative words to describe yourself?
* Is your self-talk always negative, critical and self-blaming?
* Do you blame yourself when things go wrong instead of considering other factors over which you have no control, such as the actions of other people? (We will talk more about control in Chapter 3),
* Do you have a hard time believing people when they compliment you?

The Mirror Exercise

For the next minute, I want you to say the following out loud while looking at yourself in a mirror.

I am Brave.
I am Kind.
I am Smart.
I am Strong.
I am Helpful.
I am Beautiful.
I can do Hard Things.
I am Grateful.
I am Loved.
I am Enough.

Did it feel comfortable or uncomfortable? Was it easy to do or just weird? Did you come up with other compliments for yourself, or just didn't do it at all because it was dumb? Do you think that none of the above comments/affirmations relates to you?

What is your story around your self-love? What are you making this all mean? Because I can tell you right now, you are pretty amazing, and the world needs to see your light.

Let's do some self-love building; let's start exercising that self-love muscle.

THE LITTLE GIRL IN THE MIRROR

In my study, where I am writing this and where I coach my clients, read, write and sometimes just sit and meditate, I have a charcoal drawing of me when I was maybe seven or eight years old, hanging by the door. Above it is a mirror. I look in the mirror when I walk in the door, and when I walk out, I check in with myself. How am I feeling today with me? How's the internal dialogue going? Is it positive, or I am getting down on myself about something?

The minute I feel my self-talk heading down the negative route, I look at the picture of the little girl, me, and I say those things to her. Trust me, putting yourself down when you are little is just so many ways of wrong. You catch yourself pretty quickly and stop.

If you had a picture of yourself as a little girl, would you talk to her the way you talk to yourself? Only you can answer that question.

What can you say to that little girl called you? What does she need to hear that she has never been told before?

You need to build your self-love and self-esteem muscles. Even if you don't think you have them – you do!

BUILDING YOUR SELF-LOVE MUSCLE

So, about that self-esteem muscle: it is going to take work. Here are some strategies:

1. **Positive self-talk** – talk to yourself as though you're talking to a loved one. A caring, encouraging, compassionate attitude is essential. Don't condemn yourself because of your mistakes. Remember, mistakes are just opportunities to grow and learn.

2. **Stop comparing yourself to other people** – each human being is unique and valuable in their own way. Instead of comparing yourself, recognise your intrinsic value and accept yourself, both the good and the bad.

3. **Forget the past** – concentrate on the here and now rather instead of fixating on past struggles.

4. **Don't give your worries space** – instead of focusing on anxieties about the unknown, accept you can't control everything. Don't stress about the future; be present in your current reality.

5. **Have fun** – schedule enjoyable events and activities every week.

6. **Exercise** – exercising has many benefits for your body and brain, including boosting your mood and helping with mental health. Start small to integrate it into your life – start by doing regular walks around the neighbourhood with a friend, finding a nearby gym, or making time for an activity you enjoy.

Our self-esteem plays an important role when dealing with those curveballs that life will throw our way. Having healthy self-esteem and trust in ourselves and our abilities builds our level of resilience as well.

BOUNCING FORWARD

The Cambridge Dictionary defines resilience as 'the ability to be happy, successful, etc., again after something difficult or bad has happened.'

So, when we get thrown that curveball, it is up to our level of resilience to bounce back, or as one of my coaches, Sam Cawthorn, says, 'bounce forward'. This is actually the title of one of his books. If you are a resilient person, you tend to maintain a more positive outlook and cope with stress more effectively. Like self-esteem, we can work on building our resilience muscle.

There are some people who come by resilience naturally, and others need to work on it.

Firstly, how's your social network? Do you have a strong one? It's important that you have people you can confide in. Having caring, supportive people around you can act as a protective factor during times of curveballs. Talking about the curveballs will not make them go away; trust me, I've tried. But it does allow us to share our feelings, get support, receive positive feedback and even come up with possible solutions. Seeking help from a professional may be warranted, so please do that!

It's hard to be positive when life is really testing you, but I always stop myself now and tell myself to look for the light.

Some days will be harder than others, but you know what, tomorrow the sun will still come up, and we get to have another go at it.

Some days that means having a pyjama day, or does that just happen in our household? Choose how best to look after yourself today, right now, this minute. Is what you are about to do serving you the best way?

I know that there are some of you out there who are still shaking your heads, so I want you to read the following statements and have a quick discussion in your head about how it makes you feel.

Carl Jung said, "The greatest burden a child must bear is the unlived life of its parents."

Or we can be more specific …

'The unlived life of a mother is a burden too heavy for a child to carry.'

Wow, what a punch in the guts. Our children know when we are not living our true and best life. If you are not a mother, what about your partner, your parents, your friends? What disservice are you doing them by not practising self-love?

THE ONE QUESTION TO ASK YOURSELF

Remember, this self-love stuff is hard work. It's actually a discipline of caring for YOU, the most important person in your life. It's about taking control of your life, developing self-trust and self-awareness to set the right goals, making the right decisions (learn to say NO), and understanding your strengths and weaknesses. It's essentially about being the hero of your life, not the victim, and choosing a life that feels good over one that looks good. I want you to become the person that you know you are meant to be!

A strategy I use for this is to ask myself every morning, **'What can I do today to make MY tomorrow better?'**

One of the first steps is to understand that we have a choice. We get to choose how we respond and what we can and can't control.

Katrina is sharing more in her INTERACTIVE book.

See exclusive videos, audios and photos.

DOWNLOAD it now at
www.deanpublishing.com/warrior

'God grant me the serenity
to accept the things I cannot change,
courage to change the things I can,
and wisdom to know the difference.'

Reinhold Niebuhr

CHAPTER 3
Control

So, let's talk about control.

Control was stamped on my forehead; it was my brand, my trademark. I was ALWAYS in control! Being out of control was my kryptonite. I had a ferocious need to be the best at everything, to be continually chasing approval, having been taught that perfection was the only way. As you know from the previous chapter, this was a lesson learnt very early in my life where I had been frightened to the point of perfectionism.

Then I met 'the one', the person who was *my* person, and for the rest of my life. A number of years in, the conversation started around having a family and my journey to motherhood started at around the age of thirty, about twenty years ago.

For someone who had always been in control, who mapped, planned and scheduled, I was faced with the likelihood that this getting and staying pregnant thing wasn't as easy as the entire world made it out to be; at least, it wasn't for me. *How does that happen? How come pregnancy happens to other people but not me.*

This was totally and utterly devastating to someone who had always envisaged the pigeon pair of a boy and a girl; a boy with a strong German-Austrian heritage name and a girl called Sophia, a family name.

At the time, a work colleague presented me with a poem, which I only discovered again recently. The piece of paper is just holding together. It is discoloured and its edges are frayed. I kept it in my wallet for years and would read it over and over when I needed it.

At the time, I didn't know the author's story or her motivation for penning the poem. I have since learnt that she wrote the poem in 1974 when her son Jason was born with Down Syndrome. The author is Emily Perl Kingsley, and her poem is 'Welcome to Holland'. I have included it in the appendices with her permission.

Critical analysis of the work and its influence has

compared it to the poet Robert Frost's piece, 'The Road Not Taken', which also discusses the human tendency to look back and fret about what might have been after people make decisions. I have also included this in the appendices.

Even though I hadn't read Emily's poem for over ten years, it must have stayed with me all this time.

It was clearly the inspiration for something I wrote a couple of years ago when I was trying to explain my journey to mothering the most amazing human being on the planet (just a little bias). Although the inspiration obviously came from Emily's original poetry, my heart poured these words out and helped me heal an aspect of myself I didn't realise needed healing so deeply. I am forever grateful for this journey.

I am going to share a story with you. Has anyone been to Rome? Does anyone want to go to Rome?

So, you want to go to Rome. You book your flights, your accommodation and sightseeing tours. You book into Italian conversation classes.

You look at all the pictures of Rome on the Internet, and you even download 'Roman Holiday', just one more time, because you love Audrey Hepburn.

You imagine standing inside the Colosseum, dreaming of gladiators and chariot races; you go to St Peter's Square and the Vatican and marvel at the Sistine Chapel and all of the Pope's treasures.

If you are a Dan Brown fan, you picture yourself hunting down all the clues and locations in his books. You envisage yourself putting your hand in the Mouth of Truth and waiting to see if it gets cut off. You go to the Trevi Fountain and throw your three coins in.

This has been your dream for so long you can feel it, see it and taste it.

Then the day arrives. You board your flight and begin your journey to Rome. But the Captain announces that you are landing in Paris. Paris! You didn't want to go to Paris; you know nothing about Paris. You don't know one word in French; you don't know where to go, who to see, what to eat or drink. You want to blame someone or something. Was it the airline? Was it you? Did you do something wrong, take a wrong turn somewhere? You are angry.

You begrudgingly get off the aeroplane with everyone else and find a desk at the airport that is advertising accommodation. You book a room. 'Might as well, I'm here now'. Between you and the taxi driver, you finally make it to your hotel with a lot of detours and misunderstandings along the way.

You arrive exhausted, frankly really cheesed off, feeling ripped off by the injustice of it all; you just want to crawl into bed and cry because of the unfairness of it.

But you put your big boy/big girl pants on, and you go to the front desk, indicate the maps behind the counter and go for a walk. You spend the next week walking the streets of Paris. You still shed tears at the loss of your dream of Rome, but you find many unexpected pleasures in Paris.

You have been to the Eiffel Tower and marvelled at the Gothic architecture of Notre Dame. You are surprised at the Mona Lisa's small size, and you experience the beauty of the Venus de Milo (Aphrodite of Venus).

You discover the treasures of the Musee d'Orsay, the Monets, the Manets, the Degas and the Renoirs. You peer into central courtyards and smell the blooms contained within, have coffee and macaroons at quaint little cafes. You are seduced by the flair and panache of French waiters, discover the ultimate taste sensation of a fresh croissant straight from the baker's oven and enjoy the delights of a baguette and red wine.

Then one morning, you wake up, smile and realise that you are enjoying yourself. You have discovered the pleasures and wonders of your new destination, your new reality, your new story.

This was not what you signed up for; it was not what you dreamt of, planned for, or anticipated. It has been hard and lonely and frustrating, but here now, in this moment, you have learnt that this city is just as beautiful ...

HEARTBREAK

Life is a series of decisions, and not making a decision is still a decision. We often end up in places we hadn't foreseen or even envisaged would be part of our life, but life is funny that way. We end up in a state of overwhelm, not acceptance, and Emily's poem asks us to see the beauty through the overwhelm.

I ended up being pregnant or trying to be pregnant for 12 years. The first three pregnancies ended with the infamous words many hear every day, 'I'm sorry there is no heartbeat'. Statistics tell us one in four pregnancies end in miscarriage. As someone who doesn't do anything the conventional way, each of these resulted in surgery. Our fourth pregnancy resulted in a truly amazing boy, Andreas, who makes every day a blessing and a surprise. I will introduce you to him in Chapter 9.

Falling pregnant after the birth of our son just wasn't happening. My obstetrician told me that my timing was off. Having a husband who did shift work, with me also doing shift work, resulted in us being in different places and different time zones and sometimes different countries at the times we needed to be together. This meant that months would go by without the remotest likelihood of me falling pregnant. So, my obstetrician sent me to see a specialist. We started receiving fertility help, not IVF, at this stage, but just enough intervention to get the timing right. Imagine our joy and surprise when it worked, and I fell pregnant. I was sick from day one, so I knew I was pregnant, but the biggest shock came at my first scan. My husband had stayed at home as it was just a routine scan, so I had to ring him with the news that I was very pregnant, with fraternal triplets.

Our life changed; I was so so sick with not just morning sickness. It was all day and all night sickness. I grew big quickly. I put on weight like I was eating for the entire country, which was weird as I hardly ate anything. My health started to suffer, and my doctors were concerned about me and the health of the babies. We were in and out of hospital consulting with specialists. I was a geriatric mother, and they were apprehensive about my ability to carry all three babies to term.

Their concerns were realised, and we ended up in a situation with one triplet remaining. The whole focus of us and my medical team was to concentrate on the remaining healthy baby and to take the time to mourn the other two at a later date. My membranes ruptured while on a holiday in the snow. We raced home, and I was put on bed rest in the hospital. More consultations followed with the best in the business – surgeons and professors – with entire alphabets after their names, but no one could give us a definitive answer on our baby's prognosis.

One specialist told us it was the worst situation for expecting parents to be in. Our baby was not developing in a normal way as there wasn't enough amniotic fluid surrounding it to move, breathe in, etc. Another specialist advocated for termination as our baby would die soon after birth if it even made it to term. Yet each weekly scan showed the baby still growing, and three times a day, the midwives would come into my room to check the heartbeat.

On the Friday, we decided to let nature take its course and leave it up to the baby. Two days later, on Father's Day, our baby boy, Anton, decided to come into the world too

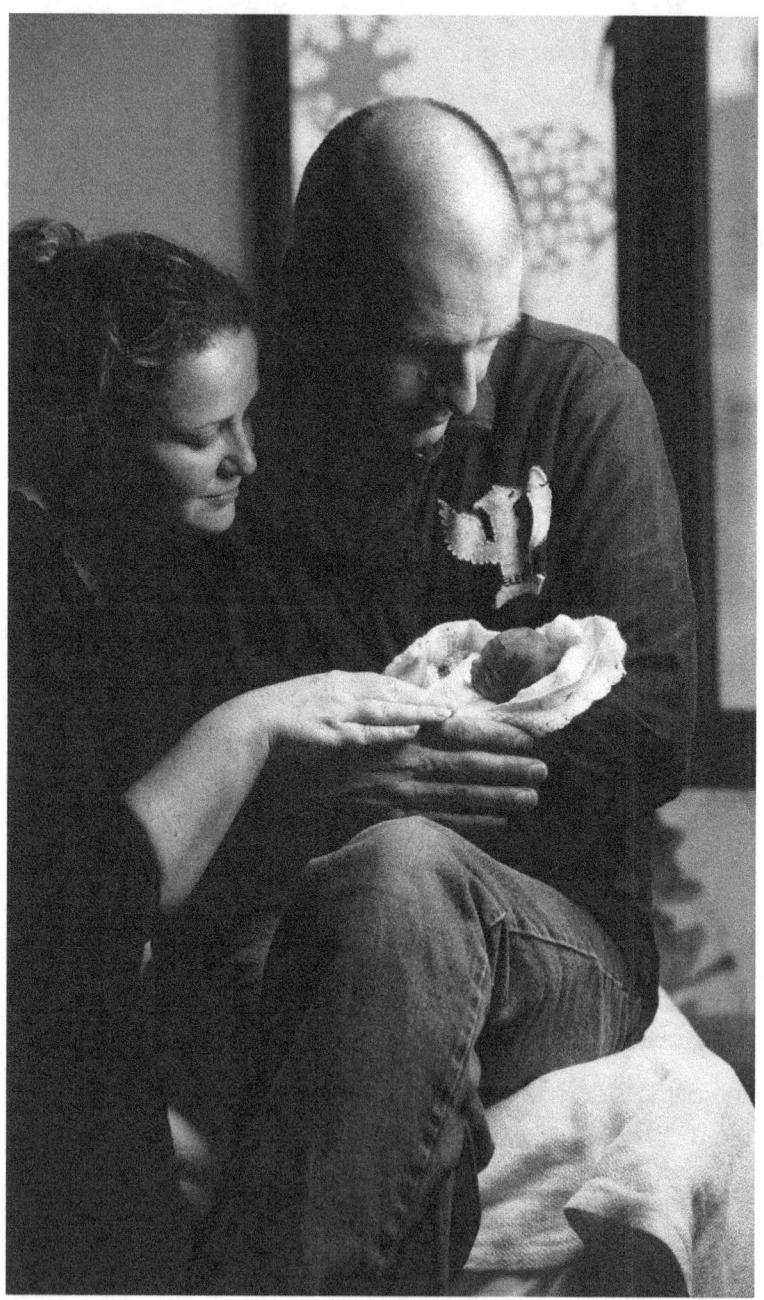

early to survive even with medical interventions. Just over 30 minutes later, he died in his dad's arms after being loved and cherished for every second of his life. I ended up in emergency surgery as I started haemorrhaging. So, on Father's Day, my brave, amazing husband not only lost his second son but almost lost his wife as well.

I spent the next week in hospital and returned home for our son's funeral the following Friday. I thought just family would be present to say goodbye to our beautiful boy but was overwhelmed by the number of people who came to offer their support. I was already in the chapel as people arrived and didn't realise that the chapel was full to overflowing until after the service had finished.

Having such empty arms, I was desperate to be pregnant again and pleaded with my husband for us to try IVF. We did, and on the second last go, I fell pregnant again. At the first scan, the doctor sent me straight to have another scan and the news this time wasn't the familiar one of 'no heartbeat'. This time, it was an ectopic pregnancy and surgery was scheduled for the next day. Overnight my fallopian tube ruptured, and the resulting surgery took a lot longer than anticipated. One more go at IVF; no joy, and my husband made the right and painful decision that enough was enough. Twelve years of reaching for the baby dream and I had achieved it. There was one beautiful boy at home who needed a mother.

Twelve years of not being able to control something that I saw come so easily to those around me. Twelve years of my body not doing what I had assumed was natural. I had run my life to this point holding so tightly to control over myself and my surroundings. Yet, I learnt a strong and powerful lesson. I learnt about the concept of control and learnt what I could control and what I couldn't, and to understand the difference.

CIRCLES OF CONTROL, CONCERN AND INFLUENCE

Stephen Covey looks at this concept in his book, *The 7 Habits of Highly Effective People*.[6] He discusses the concept of the Circle of Concern and the Circle of Influence. While we have no control over the Circle of Concern, we have control over the Circle of Influence. Covey tells us that our Circle of Concern is often larger than the Circle of Influence. For example, we can't control the climate, the price of petrol, our children's friends or our neighbours.

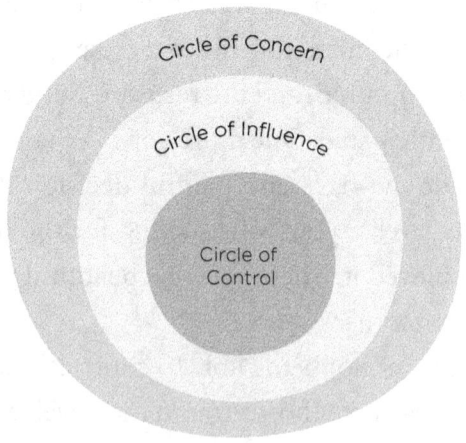

When we react to situations in life, we often become fixated on the Circle of Concern. Because we have no control over the Circle of Concern, this exhausts us, creates negativity in our life, and increases stress and feelings of helplessness. It also prioritises the Circle of Concern, which leads to the Circle of Influence shrinking as we neglect it. Yet, we seem to spend the majority of our time focused on this.

Proactive people focus on the Circle of Influence, which we have control over and can act upon. When we do this, the Circle of Influence gets bigger. When you act on your Circle of Influence, you can reduce stress levels and increase happiness because you can initiate and influence change.

Being honest with ourselves and our reactions to others, we need to ask ourselves; within which circle do I spend the majority of my time?

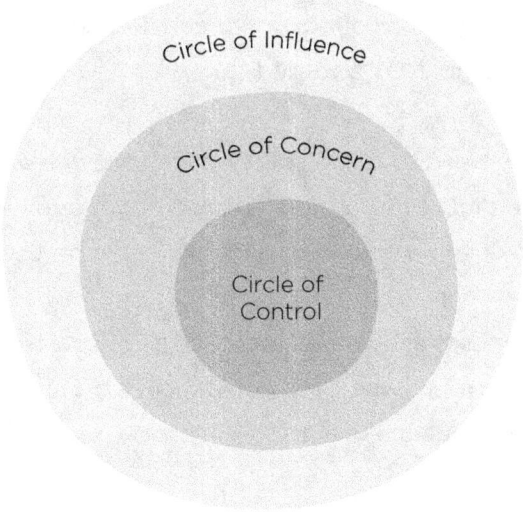

Exercise

I'm a great fan of the post-it note. As an exercise, write down on post-it notes all the things that are currently contributing to your sense of overwhelm. Or even all those jobs/tasks that you want to accomplish. They can be personal or professional. They can relate to your partner, your children, your friends, your house or even the pantry in your house. Be as specific as you can. If it's the top drawer in your kitchen where all the flotsam and jetsam goes to die, write that down. Is that just me who has one of those? You know, that drawer where the bits of string, the loose elastic bands, the sticky tape, the loose pen caps end up.

It may help by going from room to room in your house. Do a complete brain dump. Write down whatever comes up, get it all out of your head. Remember, this is a brain dump, NOT a to-do list.

You may need to make some space to lay all of these out; the dining room table is good. If you are like me, you may need a couple of pads of post-it notes!

Now comes the fun part. Distribute all the post-it notes into two groups, **the Circle of Concern group** and **the Circle of Influence group**.

CONTROL

> What can you, that is YOU, personally control? Is your Circle of Influence stack of post-its a lot less than your stack of Circle of Concern ones?
>
> What does that mean? Or a better question here is, what are you making it mean?
>
> Are you letting outside influences dictate how you live your life, or are you the pilot of your own aircraft?

In psychology, we talk about having an internal or external locus of control. Julian B. Rotter developed an understanding of the concept in 1954.

If we have a strong internal locus of control, we believe that events in our life are results primarily from our own actions. For example, getting that job promotion: we got it on our hard work and own merit, or if we didn't get the job promotion, we didn't work hard enough or didn't prepare properly for the interview.

On the other hand, if we have a strong external locus of control, we would blame or praise external factors such as not getting the promotion being the interviewer's fault or getting it only because of your mentor.

So, where do you sit? Are you an internal or external person? Are you a Concern or Influence Circle person?

Having an awareness of where we are and where we sit helps us make our decisions with clarity and intention.

TODAY, TOMORROW OR NEXT WEEK?

Those post-it notes from earlier – let's look at the Circle of Influence ones. Can they be grouped into tasks that can be done today, tomorrow or next week?

On the lines on the next page, fill them in under the headings of Today, Tomorrow and Next Week.

Pick two that can be done today. Put this book down right now and do them. Go!

Then come back and put a big tick next to those two. You are on the way.

We will use this list as we go on to talk about how you buy back your time, as this is just a start. For those overachievers, you can jump straight into using the important/urgent matrix that I will go into more detail on in the next chapter.

CONTROL

Today

Tomorrow

Next Week

'Time Management is really a misnomer – the challenge is not to manage time, but to manage ourselves.

The key is not to prioritise what's on your schedule, but to schedule your priorities.'

Stephen Covey

CHAPTER 4

Buy Back your Time

Time Management. Just the term strikes fear in hardened professionals. I don't have any time, I'm too busy, you don't understand, I have 25 children who have to walk five miles through snow with no shoes to get to school, and I have to build an ark!

So, let's look at time. Everyone has the same number of minutes in a day. I know, really! Even people like Sir Richard Branson, Elon Musk, Anthony Robbins, Steven Spielberg,

Jay Sheedy, and Oprah.

So, there are 1,440 minutes in a day, 10,080 in a week, 43,800 in a month and 525,600 in a year! But if you were just making half of those minutes count by being focused, productive and using my mantra 'living with passion, intention and purpose', imagine what your world would look like?

But first, let's look at the concept of time.

NOBODY CAN MANAGE TIME

No one can control time, but we can decide what we dedicate our time to.

1. **Time is expensive.**
2. **Time is perishable.**
3. **Time is measurable.**
4. **Time is irreplaceable.**
5. **Time is a priority.**

So, that stack of post-it notes that you have all over your dining room table – we are going to concentrate on those again. We now know what we can control the Circle of Influence ones. But again, I hear you say, I have so much to do, my list is so long. Once again, you don't understand, I have 25 children. etc.

At one stage, our son was attending three schools, all in different suburbs, one being 90 minutes away. I was coaching my gorgeous clients and working for the airline as well as being an exceptional housewife (that noise you just heard was my husband snorting in the background). I was also a slave to two pampered horses and a dog who believes that every rabbit and kangaroo (yes, we have wild kangaroos in our paddocks and around our house) is here for the sole purpose of attacking his family and way of life.

Our son was also on a machine for an hour every morning to artificially activate his non-functioning bowel and on a strict medication routine morning and night, and we needed to track every input (food/drink) and every output (do I need to explain that one, or two?). So, I get busy. I get overwhelmed, I get no hours left in the day, I GET IT! Okay.

Now, let's have a look at how we can buy back some of your time.

BUYING BACK YOUR TIME

This doesn't mean that you outsource everything, although you could. If you are anything like me and the majority of my clients, we don't have the cash to do that. I so wish! The first thing I would outsource would be cooking. I mean, why does everyone want to eat EVERY night?! I will go into my favourite activity – delegation – in more detail later in this chapter.

So, settle in. This will take a bit of work and commitment. I am not asking you to scale Mt Everest or even Mt Kosciuszko for my readers in Australia, just maybe that hill on your walks that leaves you a little out of breath. You can still talk but not sing – that type of level of work.

To know where we can buy back our time, we need to know where we spend it. Simple, right? So, I will ask you a couple of questions.

Do you know where you actually spend your time? What are you doing, who with, and why?'

Yes, or like most of us, well, sort of. I have a general idea, well, actually, not really. I just know I am really, really busy!

7 DAYS OF COLOUR CODING

For the next seven days, I want you to keep a record of what you do, ideally in 15-minute time intervals. Too severe? Okay, let's start with 30-minute blocks. I've found that the easiest way to do this is by colour coding your life.

For example:

* Work could be coded –blue
* Household cleaning – red
* Grocery shopping – yellow
* Time with the children – green
* Time with partner – orange
* Netflix/Foxtel/Stan –purple
* Social Media – black

* Time just for me (reading, massage, hairdresser, legs waxing, etc.) – pink
* Exercise (gym, walking, Pilates) – grey
* Food preparation – brown
* Family time – gold

You get the idea. Have broad topic headings, write your own, so you have a list of the major categories in your life where you spend time; basically, how your day gets filled, and colour code them.

Then draw up a quick timesheet in 30-minute blocks and keep it with you, in your handbag, in your pocket, as you go about your day and just fill in each 30-minute block as it happens. You can use apps or save it into Google calendar or the calendar on your smartphone. It can be just one word, so, looking back, you know what you mean. Now no cheating. Fill it in as it happens. If you just spent three hours scrolling Facebook, then you just spent three hours scrolling Facebook, no judgement here. This is only for you to get a clear indication of where your time is going.

At the end of each day, shade in the time blocks the colour you have chosen. At the end of the week, add up each colour block and then decide if what you are doing is the best use of your time and how YOU actually want to spend your time. This is about awareness, not judgement.

Another benefit of this exercise is accurately determining how long it takes us to perform a certain task. Human beings are noted for overestimating how much they can achieve in a day and underestimating how much they can achieve in a year.

So, the folding and ironing take twice as long as you had thought. I know, right! There are a hundred other things I would rather be doing than ironing. However, the truth is, I hardly ever iron, maybe a few tops here or there. When I first ironed my husband's, then boyfriend's shirts, I made such a balls up of it that he now does all his own ironing or sends his shirts to the drycleaners. Oops, sorry, no, not sorry. Did I intentionally do it poorly? Um, hell yes! The same with cooking, but that is a whole other story.

Regarding folding laundry, I actually enjoy this. It is my Zen time. I have one of those FlipFold boards, made famous, I believe, by Sheldon on *The Big Bang Theory*. That's where I saw it and knew I had to have one. The Container Store and a girlfriend on a trip to LA later, and I had an adult-size one and a child-size one. I love it so much I designed my walk-in wardrobe drawers the exact size to fit two tops side by side the width they come out of the FlipFold.

I love organisation, planning and scheduling. Give me a label maker and I am a pig in mud. My favourite stores in Australia are Officeworks, Howards Storage and Bunnings for storage, and any other stationary/home organisation store. In America, I can spend hours in The Container Store. I have photographic proof of my son asleep in one of their office chairs while I shopped.

While we are on the topic of laundry folding, my Zen time, I normally advocate for no multitasking, but

I will allow ironing/folding laundry to be accomplished while you are watching Netflix, but that's it. No other multitasking, okay!

I can feel some of you scratching your heads over that. No multitasking? But I am a female (apologies for the men who have tripped over this book, welcome, lovely to have you here). I can multitask, I do it all the time. Child on one hip, making dinner with one hand, organising playdates on the phone, helping the incumbent British Prime Minister iron out the Brexit deal … Neuroscience tells us otherwise. For nearly all of us, multitasking is impossible. We are wired to be mono taskers.

We actually can't do two things at once to the best of our ability and focus. Face palm, I know, really. It's common sense. The switching between tasks – don't get me started on that. There is empirical evidence that says it takes between 10 and 25 minutes to engage in a task or get back into a task after being interrupted, or trying to switch from one to another. Just thinking about that, my head hurts. How much time do we waste every day dealing with distractions and interruptions?

So, back on topic. How did you do? What stands out for you? What do you spend most of your time doing? What do you want to spend most of your time doing? Are you living your life by design or by default?

If you are living by default, let's have a conversation around that. Let's buy back your time.

So, how do we do that? Now you have an idea, where are

you spending your time? Once again, we can't manage time. It's about managing ourselves in relation to time.

We are going to go into more detail on how that looks in the next chapter.

STOP BEING THE HAMSTER ON THE WHEEL

Before we start planning and creating your dream day, we need to get rid of some of that overwhelm, the hamster on the wheel feeling. You now know where your time goes, no judgement, yet we get set in our ways, and it becomes hard to break that cycle, that habit. So, before we bring in new ideas and new habits, we need to have a clean out, a declutter of ideas and thoughts, a mental declutter. Don't worry. I will be talking more about a physical declutter later.

One tool that I love working with and use with my clients is the urgent/important matrix.

So, grab those post-it notes that you have on the items you can control, the Circle of Influence ones. You have already started by listing items under Today, Tomorrow and Next Week. We are now going to take that further.

Look at all of the items you have and decide whether they are important. These are the items that have the greatest impact on your life and have positive consequences if you do them and negative consequences if you don't.

Then, decide if the items on your post-it notes are urgent. These are the ones that require immediate attention but may be someone else's items that we have taken on ourselves and are also time related.

Give them all a score out of 10 for importance and then out of 10 for urgency.

This matrix is said to be how former US President Eisenhower organised his tasks, so it was coined the Eisenhower Principle. It is a powerful tool to organise tasks based on priorities and helps us overcome the natural tendency to focus on urgent items (putting out the bush fires). Then, it gives us time to focus on what is truly important.

The matrix has four sections. Now, put all of your tasks into the four categories on your matrix.

The ones in the **top left** we refer to as the DO NOW ones. These are the urgent and important ones, so three of these go onto your schedule, your daily to-do list.

Top Right: Not Urgent and Important, are the DO LATER ones on your daily to-do list. Once you have completed your three DO NOW tasks, you can add one or two from this category.

Bottom Left: Urgent and Not Important, are the DELEGATE ones. Oh, these are my favourites! Who can I delegate some of this stuff to? So, all those jobs piling up, all those to-do tasks, can someone else do them? Partner? Children? Outsource? (Ironing is a big one for me).

Urgent

Important

Not Important

Not Urgent

Important

Not Important

DELEGATION 101

I did say that I would mention more on delegation as it is one of my favourite activities. I have even written a whole chapter on it in a business book that I co-authored called *Back Yourself*.

Your children can do jobs/chores around the house; it's not child labour. Scientific studies have proven time and time again the many life lessons children learn by helping around the house. I talk a lot about this on my Facebook business page https://www.facebook.com/KatrinaWurmEmpowermentCoaching/, and I'm a HUGE advocate of it.

Here's a really quick summary of some jobs that children can do and the appropriate ages.

Ages 2-3

* Pick up toys
* Wipe up spills
* Dust
* Clear away their plate/cup at mealtimes
* Help unpack and put away groceries
* Sort recycling
* Put dirty clothes in their clothes basket

Ages 4-6

* All chores from the ages 2-3 category
* Make their bed
* Sort laundry and put away clothes
* Feed pets
* Make a snack
* Set the table and clear it
* Help in the garden - water plants and weed

Ages 7-9

* All chores from the previous two categories
* Get themselves up in the morning with an alarm clock
* Make their own school lunch
* Manage their pocket money
* Fold their own laundry
* Cook simple food
* Load and unload the dishwasher
* Vacuum

Ages 10+

* All chores from the previous three categories
* Use the washing machine and dryer
* Mow the lawns
* Basic home repairs
* Family budgeting (help to budget for school trips and family holidays)
* Find paid jobs for neighbours (bringing in their rubbish bins, feeding and walking animals, etc.)
* Cook a complete meal
* Wash the car.

Some other DELEGATE tasks could be ones that are not important to you but are important to someone else. I don't know about you, but I remember when my husband makes off-the-cuff remarks such as, 'oh, that would work better with a shelf there, or we should really paint this room, or that really needs fixing.' Now half the time, no, actually more like 90% of the time, I have no idea what he is talking about, and a small percentage of the time, I really don't care what colour the room is, etc.

It's not that I don't care what he thinks or wants, but to me some of these things are just not a priority. They are not on my radar. But, because he has mentioned them or pointed them out, they have gone on my to-do list. I have filed them away in the back of my brain as something that needs to be done. They have come up in my brain dump (refer back to Chapter 3 for your brain dump) and now THEY HAVE TO BE DONE! But whoa! What if you took a step back and asked the other person whether it is still a priority for them? Is it still on their to-do list? Then, guess what? It comes off your list and gets written in pen on theirs.

The final section of the matrix is:

Bottom Right: Not Urgent and Not Important. So, what do you think these are? The 'adios baby' ones. These are the ones we DITCH. Now, these may have been hanging around your to-do list or someone else's for so long but now that you have had a chance to think about them today, they are no longer relevant or needed. For example, painting your son's room with a *Thomas the Tank Engine* mural, but he is now 12, so um, totally missed that boat. Yes, I am being a little silly, but you get what I mean. Nothing feels better than crossing off stuff that is no longer relevant for your life right now. No guilt, okay? You have made a conscious decision to DITCH it, so say goodbye and move on.

Now you have a matrix with all of your tasks from your brain dump in four categories. Your Do Now, Do Later, Delegate and Ditch. The next step is to start planning your day.

Do Now (Urgent | Important)

Delegate (Urgent | Not Important)

Do Later (Not Urgent | Important)

Ditch (Not Urgent | Not Important)

CHAPTER 5

Planning

Organisation, planning and scheduling, has always been something that comes naturally to me. It wasn't something that I had to go out and learn. Tips and techniques, yes, but wanting to have control over my life and circumstances – well, refer back to an earlier chapter on that one. I remember reading a report in *Psychology Today* that highlighted that we make something like 35,000 decisions every day. If we assume seven hours for sleeping, that's 2,000 decisions every hour or one decision every two seconds. This can lead to what is called decision fatigue. I want to use my brain for more creative pursuits, not trying to make decisions every day about what to eat, wear, what schedule to follow, etc.

In addition, having children on a schedule, knowing what is happening and when, what is expected of them and when, with whom and when … I can't emphasise enough how important this is for all children, not only children with additional needs.

Having a clear household schedule is how my life works. Each member of the household knows what is happening every day and the timings around it. We have a nerve centre, which is our kitchen fridge. On it is a weekly dry erase planner, a monthly planner, meal planner, Andreas's chore chart, Andreas's reward chart (his 'catch him doing good' chart) and a dry erase board with all the important numbers from the local doctor and vet to all our closest neighbours' numbers.

Yes, Andreas does chores that he earns pocket money for. He also has jobs that are family chores. These are tasks that are done just because it is part of being a family. I am one of those people who truly believe that children need to have designated jobs in the home, from setting the table to unloading the dishwasher and cooking dinner.

YOUR CHILD'S CURRENCY

In earlier chapters, we already talked about doing a brain dump to work out your priorities, finding out where your time goes and then how to schedule your time. I have also given you the type of chores applicable to certain age groups. So now, if you have children in the house, you get to determine their chores.

This is a conversation around chores that you decide on together. Sit down with your children and determine maybe three or four weekly chores that they will earn pocket money for. If you, as a family, don't believe in pocket money, work out another reward system. I love the reward of experiences. So, sit down and discuss things that you like to do together. Let your children lead the discussion as it's their reward.

It could be experiences like going to the park to play on the swings for 30 minutes (good work out for you, so big benefit there, just saying), a coffee date one on one (works in a multiple child household). Just spending time with you, fully engaged in whatever activity your child is into at the time, can be a huge reward for them. It can be a visit to a zoo or museum or a play centre. One of our rewards was a visit to the library for as long as Andreas wanted …

Hopefully, you get the idea that the reward for chores doesn't have to result in monetary payment. It could be half an hour of battling *Super Mario Bros.*

Whatever your child's currency is, that can be their reward. What do I mean by a child's currency? And, once again, it's not monetary. A child's currency is whatever lights them up at the time. It's what they see as having the most value to them and can be an item, experience, activity, etc.

Some examples can be certain toys, video games, spending time with friends, shopping for clothes, books, going to the movies, the list is endless, and every child may have a different currency. Do you know your own child's currencies?

CHORE CHARTS

I have a really simple chore chart that I use. It has the days of the week across the top and the chores written down the side. You can buy these, or just make up your own in an Excel spreadsheet, print it out, laminate it, buy some whiteboard markers and pop it on your fridge. Then, as the chore is done, get your child(ren) to tick the chore that they did under that day. In our house, no tick = no pay.

The reason we do this is that each chore has an assigned monetary value. At the end of the week, Andreas has to add up what he has earned determined by the ticks (do you see how I have added some maths calculations there?). He has a maximum he can earn each week by doing every chore and ticking them or can earn nothing even if he had completed every chore. This gives him the responsibility of being accountable and keeping records (another sneaky life lesson I threw in).

At the time of writing this, his chores include feeding

and walking the dog, making sure the horses are fed, taking the bins out and bringing them back in, making sure his washing basket is in the laundry on a Saturday morning, then folding and putting all his clothes away. Soon he will be putting his clothes in the washing machine and hanging them out as well.

We also have family chores that have to be done because you are a member of the family and, hopefully, like living in the house, have no payment or currency for doing them. These include setting and clearing the dining room table, packing and unpacking the dishwasher and stoking the fireplace.

Today, take some time with your children to sit down and work out some chores together if you haven't got some already. Depending on your children's ages, refer back to Chapter 4 for ideas for chores if you are stuck. Now write them up on a chore chart.

Each child could have their own individual chart, or you could have just one with everyone on it. I help my clients to draw up charts for their children. You can just print out a spreadsheet you have made in Excel, laminate it, and stick it somewhere where it is visible and accessible for the whole family. I have one client who bought a large whiteboard and drew up the chart on that. Do whatever will work for your family and with the space you have available.

That's the first step to having a family nerve centre. Let's talk monthly and weekly planning. I will go into more detail on having different calendars for different family members and activities in Chapter 6, but let's talk about an overview of what I mean now.

Having your life planned doesn't mean that everything needs to be written in stone. This is just a plan, not a blood oath. You have already recorded your weekly activities in 30-minute intervals and worked out your Do Now and Do Later tasks, delegated jobs/chores to your children and ditched a whole lot of stuff, so now you need to plan to stop the overwhelm creeping in.

Looking back at your current weekly activities and considering your Do Now and Do Later tasks, what stands out for you?

Are there certain aspects of your week that you can group together, or certain aspects of your week that make sense to do at the same time? For example, if you work from home, could all the administration side of the business, the invoicing, paying creditors, etc., be done together on, say, a Monday morning? If your Do Now tasks include marketing for your business, could that all be done on a Tuesday morning?

SMART SHOPPING

What about grocery shopping? Did you find yourself picking up items on a daily basis or a couple of times a week? We had yellow as the colour for grocery shopping. I want you to do a quick exercise. We have already established that maths isn't my favourite pastime or interest, so I will make this simple (for me, not for you). On average, we shop four times a week here in Australia. On average, that shop takes one hour and two minutes (if taking children with you, it can take what feels like the term of your natural life). This includes driving to the shops, doing the shop, driving home and unpacking the groceries.

I am one of those people who put my groceries onto the conveyor belt in the order I want them packed into the bags. I even divide each bag's contents with an empty bag to make it even more obvious. Stuff for my large freezer in the laundry all goes in one bag, vegetables in one bag, pantry items all in the same bag, overflow/extra/backup items into another bag to go into overflow cupboards in the laundry, etc. You get the idea. I find this the most efficient way, and it means that when I get home, I know exactly which bag needs to go where to be unpacked. I have even toyed with the idea of colour coding the different bags … just joking, ah no, actually, I have thought about it.

Back to the weekly shop exercise. It takes 62 minutes on average for each shop, four times a week = 248 minutes a week. In a year, that's 215 hours on food shopping. Let's assume 10-hour days (once again, let's keep it simple), then that's four years of 10-hour days food shopping! WHAT?! I know! You'd better enjoy it if you are spending that much time doing it. Now you may actually enjoy food shopping, the fluorescent tube lighting, the canned background music, the piped-in food scents (to make you buy more), the bright colours … It may be your time out. If you shop at farmers markets, outdoors, in open paddocks and fields on a warm summer day with the whole family carrying wicker baskets singing and skipping along, oops, nice mental picture I had in my head. I remember a meme I once saw. It was a mother utilising Click and Collect (a service where you order everything online, a store employee makes up your order, you drive to the back of the store at a predetermined time and your items are packed into your car for you) but she had told her family she was going to do the shopping herself. She sat in the carpark and read a book until her order was ready.

So, it's up to you, do you spend four years going to the grocery shop, or do you go just once a week? I have clients who go once a fortnight. Or here's an idea, you could just order everything online. You should know by now I like a little control. So, I like to choose my own groceries, especially fruit and vegetables. But I can certainly see the appeal of home delivery, especially if you have little ones at home.

A lot of farmers markets deliver as well. Now, to be able to shop once a week or once a fortnight, you need to plan.

I have just gone into detail around one aspect of your week, grocery shopping. Can you go once a week to do your grocery shopping? Can you have a home delivery service? Remember, having a home delivery service or having someone else do your ironing or even hiring a personal chef (that's on my vision board) doesn't in any way reflect on your ability to parent or run a household, so DO NOT go down that rabbit hole.

Now that you have spent time reflecting on just one of your coloured-coded activities, take a look at the others; how could you manage them more efficiently with your time?

I will leave you to have a think about that as we now discuss meal planning!

MEAL PLANNING – HOW TO SAVE YOURSELF HOURS

The day I started planning was the day I NEVER had to hear my family ask "What's for dinner?" ever again. Massive win right there because on the fridge is a meal plan for the week. I do weekly, I have clients who do monthly, and some do two months.

The easiest way is to sit and write down all the meals you cook without opening a cookbook. Your go-to recipes, the ones you can do half asleep, holding a toddler on one hip and chairing a board room meeting via Zoom at the same time. You know those meals. Once you have written those down, ask the rest of the family what meals they like and also the ones they like to cook or can cook.

Now print out a blank calendar page. It can be a month or two months, or let's go totally wild, how about three months, or you can just go week by week. Now fill in all the easy go-to meals first, then fill in meals the rest of the family like, and then alternate them over whatever time period you have chosen. Once you have done those, you can hit the cookbooks and think about what you may want to try, and add those in. Slow cookers are the best invention ever! I remember growing up with a pressure cooker that essentially did more or less the same thing – cooked your meal for you while you could be doing other things.

Recipes can be found anywhere these days, Google search or even Facebook groups for what you may be interested in cooking. There are some amazing slow cooker Facebook groups that I must admit I can lose time scrolling through.

We have two meals a week that are pretty set in stone. Monday is make your own pizza night. Friday is fish and chips night (a family tradition from my grandparents, then parents, that may have something to do with being Catholic). So that just leaves five nights to meal plan for.

I mentioned earlier about asking your family to nominate their favourite recipes to go onto the meal plan. Here's the delegate part of that. They get to make it because you know I am all about delegating, especially to children. It teaches them life skills in the home before they are out on their own. If your children are old enough, think sharp knives. No? Actually, I have a girlfriend who produces knives for little children so that they cannot cut themselves, so no excuses.

Whatever meal your children want to eat, they can make! Think of it like this. If you have a household of four people, then that is three meals made by someone other than you. Whoever's turn it is has to write out a shopping list for all the ingredients they will need (you may need to help or guide them depending on their age), shop for those ingredients (once again with you assisting). You can even get them to budget the cost of the meal by going online to check prices and turn it into a maths/budgeting lesson as well.

You will need to assist once or twice, to begin with, or more, depending on your child's age and ability. But once they get the hang of it, you can take a step back and leave them to it. Remember, they are learning and will not do it the same way you would. Let it go. This is about you having time back and them learning an essential life skill. They may make the exact same dish each week, but hey, you didn't have to do it.

Make sure you have a list of the meals up somewhere, so everyone in the household knows what's for dinner. Remember this needs to be done before your weekly shop so everything can be included.

Then decide what day works for you as a meal prep day for the meals you are cooking. Sunday works in a lot of households. We call it meal prep Sundays – I know, a totally original name. I shop once a week. You should have already established that I do like control. I mentioned earlier that all of my groceries arrive home bagged together in the relevant bags. So, freezer items first. If I buy something in bulk, for example, chicken breasts, I divide them up straight away into enough for each meal. Pantry items are put away. I use Tupperware in my pantry, so boxes are emptied into their relevant labelled Tupperware. Using Tupperware or any clear container makes it easy to see when you are getting low on something and need to restock.

As I have mentioned, we have an overflow pantry in

our laundry, so when an item is taken out of this pantry to go into the kitchen pantry, it is added to the shopping list straight away.

Then I prepare vegetables by washing them and cutting them up. Once again, they go into Tupperware and into the fridge. That way, during the week, I can just grab the relevant containers and use the already prepared vegetables without having to chop up vegetables every night.

If no family activities are already scheduled and the afternoon is free, I will make a meal or two for the freezer. This is the time to make enough to cover at least two meals for those times when you just want to quickly heat something up that you can add either pasta or rice to. Thank you to whoever invented rice cookers; mine could permanently live on my bench. These meals are then put into freezer-safe containers labelled with whatever is inside and whether it needs something added to it, like pasta or rice. I label them because, I don't know about you, but before I did, it would be the dinner surprise while I waited for something to defrost before I knew what it was!

I also add leftover nights into our meal plan for those nights where sporting or work commitments mean that there is not enough time to cook a full meal. Some nights become soup nights, if we know that we are out for lunch with the family, and I know that no one will want to eat much once at home. So, when you are planning out your weekly/monthly plan, look at your calendar commitments and add some soup or light meal nights.

Remember, meal planning is just a plan. It's about knowing that you have the ingredients in the house to make those meals, at least for the week. Tuesday's meal can be used for Wednesday; it's okay to do that. This is also about getting rid of the what's for dinner? question as well.

Okay, that's meal planning. What about cleaning planning?

CLEAN SMARTER NOT LONGER

I have already asked you to have a look at the tasks you colour coded. How often are you washing clothes, for instance, or cleaning the house? Can you wash clothes on just one day? Or wash each individual's clothes on different days? Could you wash all bed linen and towels on another day? Without knowing the size of your family and your routines, I cannot give you specific advice. Still, I want you to be working smarter if you can, not just doing things because that's the way you have always done it. For example, I haven't washed Andreas's clothes or put them away for a number of years. He does his washing on a Saturday morning; that way, it gives it time to dry so that he can fold everything and have it put away in his cupboard by Sunday night. I never hear, 'Mum, where's my … (insert relevant clothing article)' because he has put it away, not me. Once again, I had to give up my version of how his clothes should be put away and just live with the fact that he wouldn't do it the same way as me. Like cooking, he is learning an essential life skill, and

I don't have to do it, giving me time to do whatever I want (normally, coaching).

SUNDAY SET UP

This leads me into what I call Sunday Set Up, which is one of my courses, but I am going to summarise how it works here. It comprises three parts: **Plan, Prepare** and **Organise**.

I wrote and developed Sunday Set Up for mums of primary-school-age children, i.e. children in that five to twelve age bracket (for those of you in the United States, this would include middle school).

Plan

The first step is to plan; that is having a monthly plan, a weekly plan and a meal plan. In the next chapter, I will go into more detail on how to schedule these. Part of this planning stage is, of course, filling out our nerve centre, which is on the kitchen fridge, as I mentioned at the start of this chapter.

It is essentially a combination of boards/planners that anyone in the house can glance at and know instantly what is on for that month, that week, for themselves and everyone else in the household. Each person has their own colour. I use whiteboard pens for this.

It is also where Andreas's chore chart lives – this is a weekly plan of all his chores, which he ticks as he does them throughout the week. Then there is a sheet with all the important numbers on it, emergency services, gas, electricity, neighbours' numbers, etc. These are for Andreas and our au pairs to be able to find the information quickly when needed. Think of it as what you would give to a babysitter before you go out for the night.

The final planner is Andreas's reward chart. This has a series of boxes (we have cartoon toilet cisterns – don't ask, loooong story) which he gets to tick when we catch him doing good. There are around 14 boxes to tick, and when he has ticked all of them, he gets a reward. This could be a trip to the museum, a coffee/hot chocolate date with me, etc. Doing good is when he does something nice for someone else, without the thought of reward for doing it, or when he answers straight away and jumps up to do what he has been asked, if he instantly gets off his computer when requested, you get the idea.

For some of my clients, especially those with multiple children, I help them put together whiteboards with morning, afternoon and evening routines. You can draw these up yourself or go to Etsy and get someone to make them up for you. You can also use these to keep children moving in the morning by making it a game or a challenge. Have magnets for each child that they move as they do the next idea on the list. Then, the first child who finishes doing everything to a predetermined standard gets a tick. At the end of the week, the child with the most ticks gets a reward. I don't go for physical rewards. I prefer experience rewards.

One on one time with Mum, a coffee/hot chocolate date with Dad, things like that.

This is what was on our routine charts when Andreas was younger.

Morning Routine

* Go to the toilet
* Put on dressing gown and slippers
* Eat breakfast – machine (this referred to his TES machine)
* Have medicine
* Go to the toilet
* Brush teeth
* Get dressed
* Brush hair
* PJs under pillow
* Make bed
* Pack school bag

Afternoon Routine

* Shoes off
* Unpack school bag

* Get changed
* Afternoon tea
* Homework
* Playtime
* Tidy the big room (this is what we call our playroom)
* Set the table for dinner
* Wash hands

Evening Routine

* Eat dinner
* Go to the toilet
* Bath/shower
* Have medicine
* Brush teeth
* Tidy bathroom
* 15 minutes reading
* Sweet dreams

You may be wondering about the inclusion of having him go to the toilet at regular intervals. With his bowel issues, he had to sit for two minutes after every meal to train his bowel.

Prepare

Prepare is all about preparing for the week. This is the meal prepping, cutting up all your vegetables, making a couple of meals in advance, and making school lunches. The last thing I want to be doing every morning is preparing school lunches, so Sunday is the set-up time for them. Labelled tubs in the fridge for snacks that need to stay cool – think yoghurt, cheese, items like that, labelled tubs in the freezer for muffins, pieces of cake, brownies, etc., and sandwiches and labelled tubs in the bottom of the pantry for all other school snacks. That way, each morning, your child knows to take one out of each tub, fridge, freezer, pantry, take a piece or two of fruit, fill up their water bottle, and *voila,* they have made their own lunch.

I have clients who tell me their children won't eat frozen sandwiches because they themselves had bad experiences with them as children. That is entirely up to you, but I find that, as long as you don't use wet ingredients in them, for example, tomato, you won't have an issue. They defrost by lunchtime and always get eaten. You can use sealed tubs with the items separated by baking paper or use individual resealable bags that can be reused. Beeswax wraps also work, and there are some amazing biodegradable plastic bags you can get as well. The main thing is to avoid freezer burn.

Now, you may have different ideas about what you want your children to have in their lunchboxes, maybe not a sandwich, but a wrap or something in a thermos. It can still be done on a Sunday. Set up as much as you can with your children involved. As they will be eating it, you want them to be involved in choosing what is possible.

This is all about taking away the burden on you and having them do as much as they can for themselves. It is about having a morning that is calm and organised.

Organise

Organise relates to school uniforms, or if your children do not wear a uniform, whatever they wear to school. Depending on the available space, you have two options for this step. A five-compartment sweater/jumper holder that hangs in the wardrobe or a five small drawer unit that can sit near their bed or chest of drawers. These drawer units can normally be seen at stationary suppliers, places like that. The drawer just needs to be big enough to hold clothes for that day.

So, five compartments, either hanging or a drawer unit. Label them with the days of the week. If you can find it, there is a hanging organiser that already has the days of the week embroidered on it. Then on a Sunday night, with your children's help, put the clothes/uniform for that day, including socks and underwear, into each compartment/drawer. Add in anything else that they have to take to school that day that needs to go into their bag. It may be that they need their bathers and a towel, items like that.

For all of you who do not have enough uniform pieces to cover five days, I hear you. Uniforms are expensive. I have a tip, though. If you can, and if your school allows it, try and set up a second-hand uniform swap, either a store or a Facebook Group, where parents can offer their children's outgrown items to other families. The ones I have been involved with have offered these items for free, but you can have a nominal price on items if you wish. That is how I was able to have enough pieces to cover five days, meaning I only had to wash school clothes once a week. Or more accurately, Andreas only had to wash his uniform items once a week.

Sunday Set Up is all about taking away that mad panic in the mornings to get out the door to make school on time. It teaches children responsibility for themselves and their belongings and preparing their own lunch (really just grabbing out of all the labelled tubs). This has worked for us for many years and now works for my clients as well. I love getting pictures sent to me of their own Sunday Set Up, which can also include a station by their front door where school bags and school shoes live. School mornings are a lot less stressful for mum and children because they know where all their belongings are. They know to open a drawer or take things out of a compartment in their wardrobe for that day. For mums, it gives them time to finish that first cup of coffee and be able to head into their own dream day.

'The biggest adventure you can take is to live the life of your dreams.'

Oprah Winfrey

CHAPTER 6

Your Dream Day

Huge title, I know. Your Dream Day! Some people would say, 'Imagine your day if you had all the money in the world and you didn't need to work.' What would you be doing? Where would you live, eat, drink? What would you do with your time? Ah yep, let's put our feet back on the ground and think about what your dream day will look like right now, in your current circumstances, in your current job, whether that is working outside of the home or working inside of the home (I include being a stay-at-home mum here), with your children at their current ages, your partner doing whatever it is they do. We can build the vision later but let's just be a tad realistic for now.

My current dream day is to wake up with a smile on my face because I am ready for the day. I know what is going to happen because my day is planned. I have 2–3 goals for that day that I will achieve because I know how long they will take me, and I have scheduled the time for them. I write these goals down the night before.

I get out of bed, do my morning routine (more on that later) and then love on my family by greeting them 'Good Morning.' I check the dog has been fed, walk down to see my horses and let FeFe out of her shelter. Miss FeFe, our Shetland pony, needs to eat in peace, or the big hairy Standardbred Christo will eat his food and then eat hers as well.

Breakfast is a shake with added whole fruits and vegetables in powder form (I use JuicePlus+ products) with fresh fruit added. Then it's school or bus stop drop-off, time for me to read, catch up on emails (scheduled for twice a day), lunch with friends, a client or two, a seminar/webinar or two (love learning) and maybe a presentation to a mother's group or forum. School pick-up comes around quickly, and then it's sports or code/robotics club/scouts drop-off, pick-up, dinner and night routine.

Some days are different. I might be working at night for the airline or working as a learning and development facilitator for them during the day. I could be in a product and service meeting, or I could be having a day filled with my gorgeous, delicious one on one clients.

Yes, you guessed it. My dream day is actually my present day because I have made it that way.

I know what my days look like a week, a month, sometimes a couple of months in advance because it's MY day. My life comes from what I do in MY days. Does that make sense?

I know, I know, we all have other stuff to deal with; it's not all about me, blah, blah, blah. But if you don't know what you want, once again, what are you modelling for the significant people in your life?

PLANNING YOUR DREAM DAY

When you look back on the work you did colour coding your week, how did it make you feel? Where would you like more of a particular colour or less?

So now you get to plan out your dream day. It may be that you want more orange in your week – time with your partner. Well, sunshine – if it's not scheduled, it's not going to happen.

So, go out and get whatever planning tool works for you. It can be an app or paper, A4 or even A3 size. I will let you into a little secret. As I sit here typing this, I look around my study. I currently have two yearly calendars on opposite walls and a monthly calendar on my desk to the left of my computer. As a family, we use the calendar that comes with all Apple devices. On my device, I have 15 different digital calendars that all sync when anything is changed in them. If my husband changes something in his work, personal or home calendar, I get a notification.

For example, I have an airline work calendar, a coaching work calendar (the family see that time is blocked out but no other details), a school events calendar and a home calendar – this is one where all members of the family are involved. For example, if I put something into the home calendar, every family member knows that they are expected to be at whatever the event is. Each member of the family has a personal calendar that they enter their commitments in that we can all see. They are all coloured coded, so at a glance, I know what is happening, and I also have my own colour code categories in my personal calendar.

The first step is to enter everything that is already scheduled. That is your work hours, appointments, the planning schedule you decided upon in Chapter 5, children's sport commitments, meetings at the school, etc. All the stuff you have written down on the fridge, or have reminder notes for, all that stuff –put it in straight away and colour code it.

Now, this, for me, is actually fun. If you feel like vomiting just at the thought, trust me, once you are all set up, it will get easier. For the digital ones, they all have a recurring button (so cool). If swimming lessons for the term are always on a Saturday at 10 a.m., hit the recurring button, and it self-populates!

Okay, so all the scheduled stuff is in. Now look for the white spaces, the spaces where nothing is scheduled, and you have the power to put in whatever you want!

Read for half an hour, scheduled, go to the gym, scheduled, walk the dog, scheduled … okay, so we all like a little spontaneity in our lives, or there will be days when things get off track, yes. So remember, this is a PLAN, not a blood oath.

And if there is no white space, you need to have a serious talk to yourself about your priorities and your own self-care which we have already covered. Maybe, strong hint here, you need to schedule your white spaces first! Make time in your calendar for you FIRST!

Remember, human beings think they can achieve more in a day than they actually can, so no overscheduling is allowed! Hence the reason I only want you to have three to-do items in your schedule each day. If you do these, you can look back at your list and choose another one to do.

Remember to have space for nothing as well. By that, I mean leave some white space in your schedule.

As you are filling in your schedule, whether weekly, monthly or even filling out a year schedule, remember to keep asking yourself a couple of questions. Is this how I actually want to be spending my time, the people I want to spend my time with? Are these the jobs/tasks I enjoy doing, contributing to the person I want to be? Did I say yes to what I am doing out of obligation, guilt or because I couldn't say no? You get the idea.

THE POWER OF A MORNING ROUTINE

I want you to start implementing a morning routine. It's what you do each morning to set yourself up for the day. This is to get you out of survival mode, the mad half-hour run around trying to do everything, eat breakfast, get the children in the car, find the lost sock or shoe, or homework assignment. I start sweating just thinking about it. What if I told you that mornings don't have to be like that, that there is another way?

My morning routine is about giving myself space to check in with me, physically to start with (the legacy of over twenty surgeries in the last twenty years), then emotionally and mentally. I have already mentioned that I have written down my three main goals, my Do Now goals for the day, the night before.

While I mention it, let's talk about the night before. Setting up your dream day starts the night before. On the weekend, I go through what I call Sunday Set-up, more on that in Chapter 5 . So, where was I? Yes, the night before.

How we finish a day, sign off on it, so to speak, is an excellent way to set us up for the next one. Whether you work outside the home or in it, start including afternoon/evening rituals for your conscious and subconscious mind to know it's time to wind down.

THE POWER OF A NIGHTLY ROUTINE

The benefits of sleep have been widely researched and

commented on. Good quality sleep, REM sleep, is what our body needs to restore itself. If anyone has experienced a sleep trial or sleep study, you will personally know what I mean. I have, and it was quite a weird experience. Your whole body is hooked up to sensors, including multiple ones on your head, to record your sleep patterns throughout the night. The ensuing report of how many REM cycles of sleep I had, and the actual length of sleep was fascinating. I did mine in a hospital setting, so it was very involved. Many smartwatches and fitness trackers these days can give you a breakdown of your sleep cycles as well. The one thing is, don't just look at the data you are given; look at it to see how you can improve what you are already doing.

If your mind hasn't shut down or your body doesn't know it's time to rest and restore, this will have an impact on your next day, not only physically but emotionally as well. Try a few different things, different rituals, to see what works for you.

I have already mentioned that I decide on my three to-dos for the next day. Yes, only three. I then write down anything that is foremost in my mind, maybe something that is concerning me, something I am worried about. This lets my subconscious know that if it needs to think or work on something – just one thing – while I am asleep, I am giving it permission. Thomas Edison has been quoted as saying, 'Never go to sleep without a request to your subconscious.'

Keeping a notebook and pen by your bed is also a good habit to get into. If you find too many thoughts racing around your head as you are lying there, brain dump them. Let them go by writing them down. For example, the 'I must remember to …' Write them down and take away the mental load of trying to remember them. The notebook is also good for the morning. You may wake up remembering part of a dream or an idea you want to capture, so quickly write it down. I seem to have all my best ideas in the shower. I have toyed with the idea of taking a whiteboard and dry erase pen into the shower with me to write my thoughts on the shower screen if I need to.

We have a rule in our house: no screens at least one hour before going to bed. This includes social media.

I don't know about you, but around eight hours of sleep seems to be my current sweet spot; any more or less, I become a bit cranky, and I know I do not function at my best. I say current because sleep needs do change at certain periods of our life. I'm hoping to need less and less. As a coach, I need to show up for my clients, which means I need to show up at my best. So, going to bed at least eight hours before I need to get up is mandatory for me.

Books are one of my passions, and I try to read every day. I love the feel of an actual book. So, I spend time, even if it's just fifteen minutes or one chapter, reading before I turn the light out. Yes, I was that child who would read after lights out, using a torch under the covers. Andreas is the same, and even though I grumble at him to turn out the light, I am pleased he enjoys reading as much as I do.

If I have had a particularly busy day, I also do a quick

check-in on what went right and what I learnt from the day.

Our bedroom has candles and oil reed bottles, and I change the scents for the seasons. However, my favourite scent is and always will be the scent of gardenias. They remind me of my grandmother, a powerhouse of a female, who always made me feel loved, nurtured and cared for, and it's a scent that helps me sleep. Some nights, I will also spray lavender on my pillow to help relax.

Think about your night routine. Does it help you get to sleep, or do you just fall into bed, totally exhausted, to do the same thing all over again tomorrow?

BACK TO MORNING AGAIN

Back to my morning routine – I naturally wake up around 6.30 a.m., sometimes a little earlier, sometimes a little later, but I prefer to wake up without the need for an alarm clock. I do have one, one of the old-fashioned digital ones with the light-up square numbers, on my bedside table. I do not have my mobile/cell phone in the bedroom. It is either in my study or on the charging console we have in the kitchen. We also have a no electronics in the bedroom rule. This is not only for mobile phones but iPads and computers as well. Study and work are done in the study or the kitchen at the dining room table. We are fortunate that our house is large enough for everyone to have their own study space.

I could go on to list step by step what I do, but this book is not only about me; it's about you. So, I want you to go through this with me and think about ways to start, expand or continue your own morning routine. I want you to think of a matrix, a morning routine matrix with the four sections of the matrix having the following headings: Body, Mind, Goals and Nutrition. Then, in each section, have a couple of blank lines to fill in with what you are going to do in the mornings for each of these headings.

Body: What are you going to do with your body? Stretch, walk the dog, visit your horses, have a quick dance party (check out YouTube for dance workouts you can do), do Yoga, Pilates ...

Mind: Affirmations are one of my favourite ways to clear and set up my mind for the day. I have a list of them and say them out loud to myself in my bathroom mirror every morning. Refer back to Chapter 2 for those. You could meditate, read a chapter of an inspiring biography, or just sit and use a breathing exercise for five minutes. I use the box breathing method. Sit and breathe in through your nose for a count of four, hold the breath in your stomach for a count of four, and then breathe out for a count of four, trying to expel all breath. Do this for five minutes without taking a break.

Goals: Look at your three goals for the day and decide which one is the hardest/least desirable/the one you are most likely to procrastinate on, and this one is the one you do first. Mark Twain said, "Eat a frog first thing in the morning and nothing worse will happen to you the rest of the day." Productivity consultant Brian Tracy supports this idea. Spend a morning a week looking at the whole week if you can, and schedule in other activities that will aid you in reaching your goals. Working with a coach is a great idea for one of those activities (maybe just a little bias on that one).

Nutrition: This really should be part of Body, but it is such an essential part that it deserves its own segment. I'm not going to get into a debate about whether breakfast is the most important meal of the day. I just know that, for me, my body and mind work more effectively and efficiently if I have eaten in the morning or, as I mentioned earlier in this chapter, if I have actually had something to drink, as my breakfast is a smoothie. That is, except for Sundays, as my husband makes eggs and homemade hash browns. It's a family tradition that I have carried on from my childhood, just as my Dad would do it.

As mentioned in the preceding chapter, Sundays are also meal preparation days.

I drink water with breakfast, and I know I am strange, but I don't and never have drunk coffee (I hope we can still be friends). I drink green tea with the occasional skinny milk hot chocolate. This is normally when Andreas and I have a coffee date. We call it going for coffee, but both of us actually drink hot chocolate. Too much dairy doesn't agree with me, and although we are becoming friends, too much information about that too early on in a friendship isn't wise. I think I always had an issue but since having my gall bladder removed it has gotten a lot worse.

These are just a few ideas. I want you to draw up a matrix like the one opposite and brainstorm ideas for yourself. You may already have a morning routine that works for you, so stick to it until it becomes part of you. Your morning routine is all about putting yourself first. It's about setting you up to achieve your goals, making you feel good and being intentional about what you are doing.

Part of being intentional is to also be intentional about what you surround yourself with, your physical environment.

YOUR DREAM DAY

Morning Routine

Mind
-
-
-
-
-

Goals
-
-
-
-
-

Body
-
-
-
-
-

Nutrition
-
-
-
-
-

'The best way to
find out what we really need
is to get rid of what we don't.'

Marie Kondo

CHAPTER 7

Have You Kondoed?

In 2015 Marie Kondo released a book, *The Life-Changing Magic of Tidying Up*. A girlfriend recommended it to me as being right up my alley. As you have probably realised, I love order, planning and schedules. If you stand still long enough in my house, you are likely to have a label attached to you – my labeller is one of my most used and treasured possessions. So, I went out and bought the book and slowly started using Marie Kondo's method.

However, I struck a snag – her method of determining whether or not something sparked joy. On the first day, I had thrown out the iron, the ironing board, four vacuum cleaners (Yes, there is a story there, I get vacuum cleaners for Christmas; my husband and son think it's hilarious), all the pots and pans in the kitchen, kitchen utensils, the mini exercise trampoline, the hand weights (found in the bottom of my clothes cupboard), all the presents gifted over 20 years from a relative who will remain nameless, and that was all in the first hour! My husband watching me (and his accompanying comments) almost made it out the door as well.

Seriously, though, I love her method and her Netflix series, which has opportunity and charity shops overflowing throughout the Western world, as everyone appears to be getting on the decluttering bandwagon. I see this as a good thing. In the Western world, we have come to a point where we now have storage lockers and containers to store the stuff we can't fit into our homes and lives.

We are drowning in CLUTTER. This is not only a physical problem but a mental one as well. Clutter disorganisation increases cognitive overload and can reduce our working memory. Research has shown that decluttering our physical environment has positive effects on our mental state, namely our mood. We feel freer somehow, less overwhelmed, less stressed. I have had clients who are amazed at just how much better they feel by cleaning out their physical environment and feel that a mental cleanout has been achieved as well.

Decluttering is all about getting rid of stuff to live the life you want to be living.

SO, TO KONDO OR NOT TO KONDO?

It all depends on each individual. Her practice is sound, and it works, but it's not for everyone. I do believe our possessions have 'energy'. I'm not 100% convinced on the spark joy component, but it's working for thousands of people. So, as with everything, hey, if it's working for you, keep going! Regarding our possessions having energy – stay with me here – pick up a pair of jeans or a top/shirt/jacket you haven't worn for a while and start asking yourself some questions as you hold them.

Do they still fit?
When was the last time you wore them?
What energy or feeling do you get when you hold them?
What memories do they evoke?
Good memories?
Memories of friends, family, laughter?
If they could talk, what would they say?
Do they still have a place in your life?

If I just overloaded your brain with too many questions, go simple.

For clothes just ask three: *Do I love it? Does it fit? Do I feel fabulous in it?*

Think about your environment as an extension of you. You are working on your self-love and self-care so extend that to your environment. Do those jeans deserve to be put back in your cupboard? Do they put a smile on your face, have positive energy?

Now apply that to everything you own but not all at once. A camera crew is not going to turn up at your door in two weeks to monitor your progress. It's taken you possibly your whole lifetime to accumulate all of your stuff, and probably a lot of your relatives' stuff as well, so it's unrealistic to expect you are going to be able to get rid of it all in a weekend.

Before you start throwing everything out, I want you to really think about why you want to declutter or if you actually want to at all. You may be perfectly happy with what you have. But a lot of clutter can be stuff you may have to make a decision about, and you don't want to make a decision about it. The thing is, by not making a decision, you are actually making one. Not making a decision about something is still taking up mental energy even if you don't realise it. You may have to clean it, clean around it, organise it, move it, pick it up, put it away … Everything we own takes up our time, space in our environment and our mental energy.

I briefly mentioned decision fatigue in Chapter 5. We are really only capable of making a certain number of good quality decisions each day. We have so many demands on us to make decisions, some simple decisions, some life-changing decisions, such as which high school or college to send your child to. We want our brains to be firing on all cylinders to make those big important decisions, not be bogged down by decisions over stuff!

DECLUTTERING MADE SIMPLE

There are many different methods and ways to declutter. I have already mentioned the Kondo method. Experts, courses, seminars and television shows seem to be popping up everywhere. You can only work out which method is best for you by giving it a go.

The first thing I believe you should do before you even think about decluttering is to stop buying more stuff. A good way to start this is to ask yourself a couple of questions before going to the counter to pay or clicking pay on that online shopping cart. Do I LOVE it? Do I NEED it? And my favourite, do I want to spend my hard-earned money on it? I always think in terms of my hourly rate. How many hours or minutes do I need to work to purchase this item? Is it worth my sweat and tears to get it? (just for dramatic effect, I don't sweat or cry at work).

Another tip for online shopping is to leave it in your cart for twenty-four hours. Most companies will remind you it's there via email. Just leave it there for you to think overnight whether it's something you really love, need and want to spend your money on. Someone else's money, now that's a totally different story and probably a totally different book!

As I mentioned, there are many different techniques and

styles, so I will just go through what I coach. Before you start, I want you to pick a scenario, whichever one resonates with you.

Swedish Death Cleaning. Yes, I know it sounds morbid, but bear with me. The underlying premise is that you clean out all the extra stuff so that your family doesn't have to when you die. You only keep the items you use and the items that your family will cherish once you are no longer around. 'Life will become more pleasant and comfortable if we get rid of some of the abundance,' Magnusson writes in her book, *The Gentle Art of Swedish Death Cleaning: How to Free Yourself and Your Family from a Lifetime of Clutter.*

Selling your home. Imagine in six weeks you are going to put your home on the market. You will be inviting a real estate agent around to view your home and give you a price estimation. Every real estate agent I have ever met will want your home to be clean, organised, spacious, light and airy. It should be an open book for prospective buyers to see how they can put their stamp on it when they move in. Walk around your house, viewing it through the eyes of that real estate agent. Or like The Minimalists Netflix show *Less is Now*, you can actually pack everything you own into boxes inside your house and, over a period of time, only take out what you need. At the end of the period, ask yourself if you need anything that you haven't used or searched for.

Transfer overseas. Wow, congratulations. You have just been offered that amazing life/dream job you have always wanted, and it's overseas. The company will pay for your transfer costs, which only includes one shipping container for your whole family. If it doesn't fit in the shipping container, you have to get rid of it. Anything more that won't fit, you have to pay for, and the cost is HUGE.

Or my favourite, your mother-in-law is coming to stay for a month … only joking!

These are a bit tongue in cheek but it might give you an idea of what will motivate you. Once again, you need to be clear on why you want to declutter. For me, it's because we don't need the stuff, we don't use the stuff, I'm sick of cleaning the stuff, I want to know where everything is and that everything is in its place when I need it. I would much rather be spending my time with my family having experiences, not wasting time and energy with stuff.

You want your children to remember the experiences, the time spent with you, not you not having time because you were too busy with stuff.

So, you have decided you want to get rid of stuff and declutter for whatever reason or motivation. Once again, remember this is a process. It's taken you a long time to accumulate; it's going to take time to get rid of it. And you aren't going to have a television crew knocking at your door to give you a hand, or if you do, lucky you!

CREATE DECLUTTER ZONES

I like to suggest to my clients to break tasks down into rooms or zones or types. For example, the kitchen, the kitchen and dining room (if they are one big room) or all the books in the house.

Start small, just one drawer or one cupboard. The number of people I know who have emptied their entire kitchen and been too exhausted at the end of the day to put it all back. And then it stays like that, and they work around it for a day, then two days … If you find it just starting to become overwhelming, ask a friend or family member over to help. I have spent many delightful evenings at friends' houses, helping them to declutter with a glass of wine in my hand. Oh, I should point out, I help clients with the mental act around decluttering; I don't physically turn up at their house to do it, even though I have been offered obscene amounts of money to do just that.

Maybe set a timer, and whatever you can do in 15 or 30 minutes, do just that. Remember to always finish what you've started. Take what you are throwing out and put it straight into the bin. Put the bags you are donating straight into your car and even drive to the charity shop that day. Do not drive around for months with stuff in your car that you are donating. Do it that day or at the latest that week.

But what if I need it, want it, can use it SOMEDAY? Yes, I see you procrastinating over those what-if items. Someday is not today. Only have items in your house that you use every day, items that you enjoy. Nothing is too special to only use on special occasions. Today is a special occasion. You are breathing. You are alive. Make every day a special day. We don't know what tomorrow will bring, so today is where it's at. Use those crystal glasses, those wedding present plates. Enjoy the stuff you have today.

If you think you may use something in the NEXT SIX MONTHS ONLY, then okay, hold onto it, as long as it has its own storage place, and you know where it is. If you don't think you may use it in six months, then get rid of it. If you need whatever it is after you have gotten rid of it, ask someone if you can borrow theirs. Or the newer, latest and greatest version might be on the market, and you can buy it.

Some good questions to ask yourself as you pick up each item. I mentioned earlier that the spark joy thing is not me. I get it, but it's not me. But I do pick up each item and ask myself the following questions: How long has it been since I used this? Do I like it? Does it work properly? Is it broken? Does it fit? Do I have more of this? How much/many do I need of this? If I keep it, what will I get rid of to make room for it? Does it have a designated place, a home where I can locate it instantly and easily? And for paper, manuals, etc., can I find this online?

WHY I DON'T RESELL MY 'STUFF'

You may have noticed that I only mention getting rid of items. Getting rid of stuff can be putting items in the rubbish, donation to charity, giving them to someone else or selling them.

I don't advocate selling stuff, but that's entirely up to you. I have used the item, enjoyed it, and now it's time for someone else to enjoy it. I know this is hard, especially for items that cost a lot. I think of it like this. My time is my most valuable resource. My time is precious. I can't get it back. If you add up the time to take photos of the item, post it online somewhere, respond to the enquiries, wait around while people turn up or not, it takes too much valuable time. I would much rather be doing something with my family. My time is worth too much to be wasting it selling stuff.

When I cleaned out the toy room, there would have been thousands of dollars of stuff. So, I contacted all the mothers in my street with younger children and offered them whatever they wanted. I then invited teachers, including the vice-principal from the local primary school, to see what they could use, and they took the rest. It took no time at all. I didn't have to drive anywhere. I knew the people who came into my home, and we had a social visit at the same time. I felt good because I knew everything would be appreciated and enjoyed by other children.

We have a list of family values, and some of them are contribution/altruism and giving/donating. I see it as a part of this.

START WITH ONE

If you are still finding it difficult to start, try with just one item, then tomorrow just two items, and the third day three items. Do this for a month, adding an item a day. By the end of the month, if it has 31 days, you will have cleaned out 496 items. This method is the one used by The Minimalists. You can visit their website at www.theminimalists.com/game/.

You can also search Google for decluttering lists; trust me, there are thousands of different ones you can print out and follow if you want more direction. I think the last time I looked, there were almost 850,000 results. I find Pinterest to be the best when searching, and people make such pretty, colourful ones.

It's like anything – if you want your home environment to be clutter-free, your life to be different, your circumstances to change, YOU actually need to do something about it. You need to take some form of action, even if it is to hire a decluttering expert or service to do it for you. You need to have a vision of your life and a plan to achieve it. This is your life. No one is going to live it for you, or better yet, don't let anyone live it for you!

Here is a famous quote by Greg S Reid,

> 'A dream written down with a date becomes a goal.
> A goal broken down into steps becomes a plan.
> A plan backed by action makes your dreams come true.'

Let's talk more about action, particularly something that has become a bit of a coaching mantra – The Law of Attraction.

'Whether you think you can or think you can't, either way you are right.'

Henry Ford

CHAPTER 8

The Law of Attraction and all that *frou-frou*

The Law of Attraction is a philosophy that believes if you focus on something, you can attract more of it to you. It has been taught in different versions and manifestations throughout history.

I mentioned back in Chapter 1 that I would love to be able to give you a magic pill for you to have everything you want in your life so that you could just sit on your couch, and everything you wanted would somehow just land in your lap. I do wish this for you, but I live in the real world.

I strongly believe in the power of activating your reticular activating system. Let me explain that by using the metaphor of buying a car. Hopefully, like driving a car, you have looked at buying a car at some stage in your life, whether new or second hand. So, you go through the process of visiting car dealers. You look at different makes and models and decide on the one that you want, maybe even decide on the colour.

I love my car. When I finally decided to purchase this car, I wasn't that familiar with it. I didn't know anyone who had one, but the safety features won me over, and it looks pretty good as well. I loved it so much that when I got a new one, I got the same make and model as my previous one.

After I made the decision, everywhere I went I saw 'my car', the particular make and model, everywhere. I couldn't drive anywhere without seeing one. Why was it that I hadn't seen them before as they had obviously been there? This is the reticular activating system (RAS) in play. Our brain has been alerted to something, so then keeps looking out for it, whereas before, it wasn't even on our radar.

Let's tie this back to the Law of Attraction and start with that ever-present emotion that every mum deals with, or at least every mum I know among my family, friends and clients. Guilt.

MUM GUILT

So how does Mum Guilt (yes, I am using capital letters because it needs a capital letter!) tie in with the Law of Attraction? The Law of Attraction was one of those things that you read about in self-help books, the whole personal development guru-speak thing. I'm a logical, pragmatic, yes sometimes a pain in the butt person, or can I say pain in the ass (sorry to those of you I just offended by my use of the word 'ass', oops, said it again), because I believe, if you actually want something, you need to take action.

Maybe the thought that I was personally responsible for all the stuff – the good and the bad that had happened to me – was a little too confronting, especially the bad. So, I dismissed the whole Law of Attraction concept. Like, really, was I manifesting all of the heartbreak and devastation that periods of my life had become? Who would want to do that? But, through opening myself up to the possibilities and the realisation that there are other universal laws (I will get to those later), I started to manifest what I wanted. I know, who knew?

This was evident when I arrived at my son's academic scholarship presentation at the exact moment his name was announced for him to go up on stage to receive it.

But let's backtrack to a couple of days before. I live in Australia, and my son's presentation was on Monday at 9.30 a.m., with morning tea afterwards. It was at the high school that he was about to attend. He had gone through the scholarship application process, testing and an interview and gathered evidence for the application submission. We were extremely proud when the high school principal rang to say they were awarding the school's academic scholarship to Andreas. Woohoo, no school fees! Seriously though, my first thought was, oh no, we won't be there to see him receive it.

I would be coming home from New York via Los Angeles, scheduled to land back in Melbourne at 9.30 a.m. that actual morning, and my husband would be in Singapore. So, I quickly contacted his primary school principal to see if she could take him and did a Facebook shout-out to any mothers attending the awards morning (who already had children at the high school) to ask if they could please video Andreas as he walked on stage to collect his scholarship and be presented to the high school community.

So, Mum Guilt alleviated just a little bit, but I still felt horrid. My husband and I told Andreas that he had been awarded the scholarship, but unfortunately, we would be unable to attend the awards morning, where he would be presented with it. I even offered to stay home and not go to New York, but this kid, who amazes me every day, turned around and told me that I had to go to New York as I was a finalist in the Stevie Awards.

So, back to that Monday morning. Oh yes, I glossed over that in the previous paragraph. The Stevie Awards are considered the world's premier business awards. They were created in 2002 to honour and generate public recognition of the achievements and positive contributions of organisations and working professionals worldwide. I was a finalist in their Women in Business Awards. The award ceremony was on the Friday night before Andreas's awards morning. I was honoured to receive a bronze in the Women Helping Women Category for my coaching services. Now back to Andreas.

On the flight from Los Angeles to Melbourne, I was not only upgraded to business class (flat beds – the only way to travel) but found myself seated next to a beautiful girlfriend who had been to the States for work. So, two major plusses right there. On the flight, I took out the draft of this book and thought about this exact chapter, The Law of Attraction and the other universal laws. I decided to go straight to the high school after I landed to attend the morning tea after the awards were presented. That way, Andreas would know that I had made an effort and wanted him to know how proud I was of him. So that became my goal. I went through each step of the process in my mind: disembarkation, customs and immigration, bag carousel, quarantine and then out of the terminal where our current au pair would be waiting to pick me up in a designated prearranged location. I visualised each step in detail.

We landed, and my plan went into action. It was like a military operation, off the aeroplane, straight through customs, my bag was fourth out on the baggage carousel (when does that ever happen?), waved through quarantine, outside … to wait ten minutes for the car, the car arrives, jump into the driver's seat and drive to the high school. I promise no speed rules were broken (my fingers may be crossed behind my back writing that, but you can't see them, and to my two nephews who are policemen, you didn't read that!). I drove up to the school's gymnasium where the award morning was, double-parked, jumped out of the car, leaving it running for our au pair to drive it to a parking spot. I ran into the back of the gymnasium to hear, 'The Academic Scholarship this year goes to Andreas Wurm' literally the minute I ran in. What?! I know, crazy right?!

In the next break between awards, I walked up the aisle to the second row where Andreas was sitting with his primary school principal and slid into a seat next to them. Andreas just took my hand and stared at me for a good five minutes as if to ascertain if I was truly there or not.

Exiting the gymnasium at the end of the ceremony, the high school principal saw me and asked how I was there as he knew I was on an aircraft. All I could reply with was, 'I don't know, but everything lined up, and I made it just as you called Andreas up to the stage.' I also mentioned that maybe he didn't want to get too close as I had been travelling for over 20 hours, but he said he was 'all good' as he had a cold. So, HUGE Mum win! Mum - 1, Mum Guilt - 0!

VISUALISATION AND MANIFESTATION

So, that visualisation, that energy I was projecting, amounted to taking action, resulted in what I wanted. I wanted our son to know that I moved heaven and earth to get to his award morning because it mattered, and he matters. But, like I keep saying, you can visualise or even create a vision board. You can have a daily mantra or tell yourself a positive affirmation every day, but you also need to take action.

So, what are you creating or manifesting in your life?

I love neuroplasticity and the idea that what we tell our brain our brain believes. I mentioned the RAS earlier in this chapter. But for it to stick, for it to truly manifest, you need to do the work.

So, let's talk about vision boards. I love them and recommend them. If you don't have one, let's make one.

VISION BOARDS

Vision boards are powerful because they help us to attract things into our lives. You still have to do the work, though! A vision board is really just a daily reminder of why you need to keep showing up every day until you achieve that vision, so it has to be somewhere you will see it every day.

There are a number of ways to do a vision board. My favourite is to buy a big empty frame, grab some scissors and glue, a heap of magazines (with things inside you aspire to) and photos as well.

Then look at the goals you want for your life in each of the three areas of health, wealth and relationships. You can add in dreams as well, whether travel, a new car, a nice little 1969 Mercedes 280SL would be nice, a villa on Lake Como … sorry, where were we? I got off track for a second.

Now get creative. You can add in quotes. Just have fun

and think of all the things, experiences and opportunities you want to attract into your life. It could be more time with friends, so add a photo of your friends. It could be a job promotion. Let yourself dream big.

Make it a real statement of YOU, the you that you are becoming, the you in twelve months' time, or five years' time. When you look at your vision board every day, you feel excited, energised, happy, content. It lifts you up. It's your vision.

So now you have your vision board up, in a place where you will see it daily. Break it down into steps to achieve those goals.

At the start of the chapter, I mentioned that the Law of Attraction is one of the universal laws, so I thought I would give you a quick summary of the others.

Different sources quote different laws, but I like the 12 laws. I find they sum everything up very nicely.

1. **Law of Divine Oneness** – this is that we are all connected. So, what we think, say and do will have an effect on others and the universe around us.

2. **Law of Vibration** – everything in the universe moves and vibrates. The same principles of vibrating in the physical world also apply to our thoughts and feelings. Each sound, object and thought has its own vibrational frequency.

3. **Law of Action** – I think you all know how I feel about this one. We must engage in actions that support our thoughts, dreams, goals, emotions and words.

4. **Law of Correspondence** – this is related to the Law of Divine Oneness. Throughout the universe, there are repetitive patterns. Significant patterns can repeat on smaller scales.

5. **Law of Cause and Effect** – nothing happens by chance or outside of these laws. Every action has a reaction or consequence.

6. **Law of Compensation** – the old adage of you reap what you sow. What you put out into the world will correspond with what you receive from the world.

7. **Law of Attraction** – in brief, we create the things, events and people that come into our lives. Our thoughts, feelings, words and actions produce energies, which in turn attract like energies.

8. **Law of Perpetual Transmutation of Energy** – now that's a mouthful. This means that everything around us is in a constant state of flux, and higher vibrations can affect lower vibrations. The best way to understand this one is when you are feeling low, being around someone who is happy

and encouraging to you can lift you up, therefore changing your vibration.

9. **Law of Relativity** – there is a saying that if you are with a group of friends and you all put your problems in a basket, and everyone got to choose which problem they would take out, everyone would take their own back. This law is about comparing our problems to others with a proper and clear perspective. No matter how bad we perceive our situation to be, there is always someone worse off; it's all relative.

10. **Law of Polarity** – everything has an opposite. The existence of opposites help us understand our lives and help us be resilient in hard times – the old silver lining adage.

11. **Law of Rhythm** – linked to the Law of Vibration but opens it up more, in that not only does everything move and vibrate, but everything also has cycles as well. Think of the seasons, the body's aging process, a season for everything and everything has a season.

12. **Law of Gender** – no, not talking about whether you are a female or male. This is about the fact that there are two types of energy, masculine energy and feminine energy, and we all possess some amount of each. It's finding the balance between the two.

IT'S NOT ALL MAGIC

So, if you want something to magically appear in your life – sorry, sweetheart. I so wish I was a genie like the one in *I Dream of Jeannie*, a TV show from the late '60s, and could grant your wish and then transform into smoke and go back into my bottle. If you have no idea what I'm talking about, Google it!

So, for those coaches out there relying on marketing just around the Law of Attraction, shame on you. You are setting up a false expectation for your clients, and that's not fair.

I met a coach once at a networking event who mentioned that she tells her clients that they can have anything they want. Anything? At the time, I was working with a client whose son was non-verbal. All she wanted in the world was to hear her son speak. Now I would never assume to tell her that all she had to do was rely on the Law of Attraction and that it would happen. No, that's not how it works. As we worked together, she investigated specialists who had worked with children in a similar situation to her son. We researched different technologies available, and she put hours into research and appointments. And yes, she did hear her son speak through the aid of technology, but boy, did she have to work for it.

You, my gorgeous reader, as I mentioned at the start of this book, are going to need to get off that couch (lounger), put down that drink and get moving. Get clear on what you want, get clear on whether it is achievable for you, and if not, why not? What do you need to be able to achieve that goal? Is it information, mentoring, money, a coach to hold you accountable? Dreams, goals, habits … they take work. No one that I know has ever truly been an overnight success.

I mentioned getting clear on what you want; you also need to get clear on your WHY. The reason you want to do those things, the reason for your passion, your reason for getting up and to keep pushing on those days when you think you can't. My WHY is my boys, my husband Michael, our son Anton and our son Andreas who I will introduce you to in the next chapter.

'Here's to the crazy ones.
The misfits.
The rebels.
The troublemakers.
The round pegs in the square holes.
The ones who see things differently.
They're not fond of rules.
And they have no respect for the status quo.
You can quote them, disagree with them,
glorify or vilify them.
About the only thing you can't do is ignore them.
Because they change things.
They push the human race forward.
And while some may see them as the crazy ones,
we see genius. Because the people who are crazy
enough to think they can change the world
are the ones who do'.

Rob Siltanen

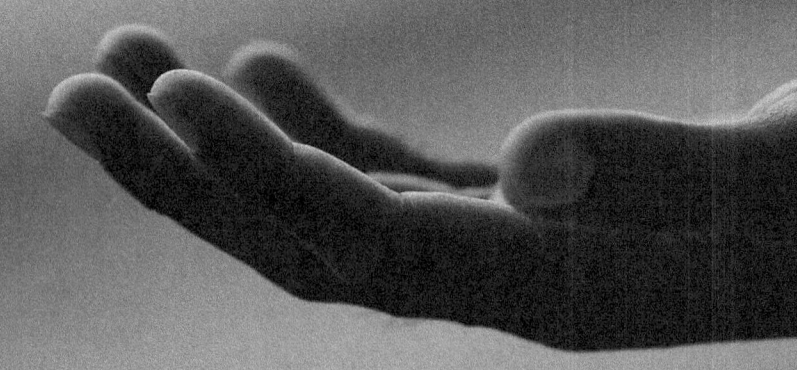

CHAPTER 9

Welcome to Motherhood

Introducing my Boy: My WHY

I want to start this chapter with my thoughts on what parenting looks like. It could look like someone with one child, someone with ten children, someone with stepchildren, or, you know what, someone with no children, but is a great aunt, uncle, friend, godparent or grandparent.

If you have interactions with children, where you are responsible for making decisions on their welfare and upbringing and are there at the coalface parenting, then hey, in my view, you're a parent.

Also, a big hug to those of you who wanted desperately to be a parent, and through whatever life circumstance, you couldn't.

I see you, and I feel for you.

There are many views on how to parent. I've heard many different terms and buzzwords. Helicopter parenting (I was once told that this described me), concierge parenting, free-range parenting, snowplough parenting, hands-off parenting … and the list goes on.

I like Diane Baumrind's definition of parenting styles. She states that there are four distinct styles. They have distinct names and characteristics and vary in at least four areas: discipline style, communication, nurturance, and expectations.[7]

They are authoritarian or disciplinarian, permissive or indulgent, uninvolved and authoritative.

Authoritarian parents are the ones we would say are the **disciplinarians**. They use a strict discipline style with little negotiation, and punishment is pretty common. They communicate with their children by talking at them, and rules are usually not explained, just enforced. They are typically less nurturing and have high expectations, with minimal flexibility.

Permissive parents are those who are more like friends than parents. They let their children do what they want and offer limited guidance and direction. They tend to be warm and nurturing and have an open communication style where the children get to choose for themselves and figure out problems independently. Expectations are not normally set by this type of parent, but if they are, they are minimal.

Uninvolved parents give a lot of freedom to their children and stay out of their way. This can be a conscious parenting choice or could be that they are less interested in parenting or unsure of what to do. There is no particular discipline style. They mostly let their children do what they want, whether through lack of information or caring. Communication and nurturing are limited, and they have few or no expectations.

The final one is the **Authoritative parent**. These parents are reasonable and nurturing and set clear high expectations that include input from the children. Their children tend to be self-disciplined and think for themselves. Disciplinary rules are clear, and the reasons behind them explained. Communication with their children is frequent and age appropriate. This style is thought to be the most beneficial to children.

So, if one of these definitions resonates with you, go for it. Remember that it is unlikely that you will parent in just one way and may use a combination or even different styles at different times. What works for a five-year-old may not work for a fifteen-year-old. Only you know what's best for your family and your children.

THE GIFT OF LOVE AND REALITY

When our son Andreas was born, we were ecstatic and then reality set in. I sucked (was hopeless) big time at this mothering thing. No matter how hard I tried breastfeeding, it was jaw-clenchingly, stomach-churningly painful, and this is from someone who walked around for two days with a burst appendix.

Visits to lactation consultants made me feel worse as it appeared to be my fault, my lack of skill in the baby's correct positioning. Deeper into the depths of despair I went.

I had a baby who slept for a maximum of twenty minutes and then screamed for what seemed like all of his waking hours. I was on edge, questioning every decision I was making. And then the panic attacks started. I would be frozen solid, sweating, pain in my chest and totally overwhelmed. The trigger could be a simple journey to the shop and the fear they would be out of a particular brand of nappies or baby wipes.

I concluded that I had totally wrecked my life, my husband's life and my poor baby's life. I just couldn't do this mothering thing. I could control, and did, every aspect of my life to this point (once I became an adult), but this baby wasn't following any book I had read – and I read everything I could lay my hands on. If reading 20 books per week makes you an expert on something, I was up to PhD level. Book Depository would have made their yearly profit just on my orders.

But nothing fitted; nothing took hold. I tried all of the recommendations, back and forth to the local doctors. I would try something else, back and forth to the maternal health care nurses, try something else. Then the local maternal health care nurse, the one that I felt the most comfortable with, told me to stop trying to breastfeed and try formula, especially now that our baby was losing weight. The weight of failure again pounded me into the ground.

So, we started with formula. My husband even bought a formula machine, like a coffee machine, but for formula. You added a tin of formula into the top and filled up the water reservoir. You turned it on. It sterilized the bottles, heated the water and mixed the formula into the bottle. It had a chamber for the empty bottles as well. The only thing it didn't do was put the teat and lid on.

Still no change. So, I decided that this child needed a new mother as I clearly wasn't cutting it. I ended up at a girlfriend's house shattered and in tears, handed her the baby and told her to take care of him. She immediately rang my doctor, and I was admitted straight away into a Mother and Baby Unit at a private hospital.

I was diagnosed with severe postnatal depression, and for the first three nights, the nurses looked after our baby so that I slept. Confirmation was bittersweet as they couldn't settle him either, and so our journey began to try and figure out what was going on.

Silent reflux was the diagnosis, and treatment started. The first two medications they tried didn't work. So, another was tried. This appeared to work as he stopped screaming. I was still asking questions regarding his bowel movements and how infrequent they were and was told time and time again that variations were normal and not to worry.

Antidepressants were prescribed for me, and my panic attacks lessened and then stopped. I was allowed out of the unit and was able to go for walks, firstly just by myself and then taking our baby with me. I lived in that unit for almost three months the first time. Yes, you read that right, the first time. I went home, and because I didn't have an ongoing support structure in place, the panic attacks started again, and I was readmitted. This time, before I was discharged, I needed to have childcare organised and in place.

So, family day care was organised as well as a childcare centre to give me time away from the baby to rest, recover and take care of myself, whether just going for a walk or reading a book.

Life settled into a rhythm, and my organisation and scheduling personality kicked back in. The household settled into a routine with aspects of my life on autopilot. I needed to get myself back out into society, so I started working at a local café to get comfortable with people again before returning to the airline after my maternity leave came to an end.

The bowel issues of our son continued to puzzle me, and toilet training was just not happening. He flatly refused to wear underwear and always insisted on a nappy and then a pull-up. At childcare, he wasn't being graduated from room to room as he still wore a pull-up. He couldn't move up as the requirement to graduate to the next room was that he had to be toilet trained.

Our paediatrician couldn't explain the fact that our son couldn't or wouldn't be toilet trained. We had tried all of his suggestions and recommendations, and he admitted defeat. We informed our son that he had to wear underwear if he wanted to move into the kinder room at childcare. His response was to ask at which age was he required to do that? We told him at age four.

So, on his fourth birthday, he put on underwear and walked into the kinder room. I remember asking why he persisted with nappies or pull-ups for so long. 'If I wear nappies, I can keep doing what I'm doing, and then you change me. If I have to go to the toilet, I have to stop doing what I'm doing, to go.' But we still had issues with his bowel. He continued to have accidents and would tell us that he had no sensation of it happening.

Back to the paediatrician, and x-rays were taken of our son's bowel. It appeared to be impacted and full. We ended up in the rooms of Dr John Hunter, a developmental paediatrician, and that's when the fun really started.

Before going down the behavioural road of why Andreas was having such trouble with his bowel, Dr Hunter arranged for us to see a range of specialists at the Royal Children's Hospital in Melbourne, Victoria. He was also curious about the size of Andreas's head as Michael and I had fairly normal-sized heads, and Andreas's was particularly large.

The first specialists we saw were Professor John Hutson, the chair of paediatric surgery at the University of Melbourne and one of the consultant paediatric urologists at The Royal Children's Hospital, and Wirginia Maixner, a neurosurgeon and Director of Neurosurgery at the Royal Children's Hospital.

Both of them decided to start testing. So, it began, a nuclear colonic transit study on his bowel and MRIs on his head. The results came back. Firstly, a diagnosis of slow transit constipation.

'Slow transit constipation (STC) is a chronic disease of the colonic muscle in which an abnormality of the nerve fibres makes the colon unable to function properly and move the body's waste through the digestive system. Irregular stool output (impaction) and faecal overflow may occur as a result (yes, we had figured that one out). While the disease can progress rapidly and be life-threatening (something every parent wants to hear – not), it can be stabilised, with treatment being transdermal electrical stimulation, using an interferential therapy machine (TES), and oral medication.'[8]

Then we received the results from the MRI scan. A diagnosis of hydrocephalus.

'... there is longstanding moderate tetraventricular hydrocephalus in association with a Blake's pouch cyst of the posterior fossa.'

Okay, so what now? Armed with these reports, what does any parent in this situation do? Go to Google and start researching and get more and more concerned and overwhelmed.

'Hydrocephalus is the abnormal enlargement of the brain cavities (ventricles) caused by a build-up of cerebrospinal fluid (CSF). Usually, the body maintains a constant circulation and absorption of CSF. Untreated, hydrocephalus can result in brain damage or death. There is no cure, but hydrocephalus can be managed with surgery.
　CSF is a clear fluid that is made and absorbed by the brain. CSF circulates through the cerebroventricular (brain cavity) system and then through the subarachnoid space that surrounds the brain and spinal cord. It serves to protect and nourish the brain and spinal cord.'[9]

So back to Dr John Hunter to find out where to from here. More testing was recommended. He sent us to Professor George Werther, a paediatric endocrinologist, who conducted a bone age scan as Andreas was under height for his age.
　Wirginia Maixner sent us to Professor Vicki Anderson, a paediatric neuropsychologist and Head of Psychology, to

determine the impact on his neurological development and functioning. She also sent us to Associate Professor James Elder, a paediatric ophthalmologist, to check the pressure, if any, the hydrocephalus was causing.

Professor Hutson enrolled Andreas into a specialist programme at the Healthy Bowels Clinic at the Royal Children's Hospital and sent us to Professor Yves Heloury, a paediatric urology consultant, for a consultation.

Let me just take a breath. I'm exhausted just writing all of that down. You can imagine what our life was like over months of going back and forth to the hospital while all of these tests and appointments were taking place.

Andreas coped extremely well, and we took our lead from him. He asked pertinent questions and wanted to know what he was being tested for and why. We made sure he was involved in all aspects of his treatment and care.

So, at the end of the initial flurry of specialists, testing, meetings and follow-ups, we had an outline of what we were dealing with and how our lives would look.

Compensated (arrested) hydrocephalus. As he was not experiencing symptoms, Wirginia took a wait-and-see approach with regular monitoring, with treatment possibly required at some point. She explained that if they operated based on scan results, Andreas would have been in surgery straight away, but because he was obviously living a full life despite the hydrocephalus, the wait-and-see approach was the best decision moving forward.

Slow Transit Constipation. There was regular monitoring

at the hospital bowel clinic, fortnightly to start with. Gluten and dairy were eliminated from his diet. The Interferential Therapy Machine (TES) was attached every morning for one hour, and a healthy bowels daily flowchart showing all food and drinks and the time they were consumed had to be completed. All medicine, the timing of the TES machine, all output (no explanation needed) using the Bristol Stool Form scale, pain level, a feeling monitor (irritated, happy, surprised, worried, sad or angry) and whether any leakage 'sneaky poos' had happened, was recorded. There was also a section on the chart to fill out if there was anything else to report.

So, our new normal began.

The meeting with Professor Anderson opened up another can of worms. Dr Hunter had been the first doctor to openly use the word gifted when he referred to Andreas. The local doctor had mentioned in passing that he was very bright, and we had early indications that he was certainly not following the prescribed path of learning milestones written and talked about by other parents.

He was reading early readers at the age of two, doing jigsaw puzzles upside down and asking for an old computer that had been donated to the toddler room at childcare to be fixed. His exact words at eighteen months old to one of the childcare workers was, 'Anti (Antoniette) the computer is broken, can you fix it please?' Childcare called us in to talk about his development. We knew that he was bright, but until the testing performed by Professor Anderson, we didn't know how far off the right-hand side of the bell curve he was.

The testing was done early. He was five, as Wirigina wanted a baseline. Traditionally, IQ testing is not performed under the age of seven.

We took the results back to Dr Hunter. He sat us down and explained that, while Andreas would not need the education provided in primary school, he would need the emotional and social learning that comes with being with his age peers.

He outlined that, in the past, children like Andreas would be at university in their early teens but found the lack of emotional and social maturity crippling, impacting their mental health. It is also hard to get a position in any field as a university graduate at 15 years old.

So, after I stopped crying, my research started. I think I cried for two weeks straight. Michael couldn't understand why I was so upset at Andreas being gifted. I was so hoping for him to be bright and talented, not gifted. The reason I was so upset was because I knew. I knew what it would mean. I knew the challenges, the bullies, the misunderstandings, the feeling of always being in the wrong place at the wrong time, the out of body experiences when people didn't follow the rules, when people didn't stick to their word, the huge emotional intensity of pure empathy with others, the exhaustion of being in a crowded, noisy room.

I got it because I am gifted. I got it because it was and is my life. I got it because I spent my school years being bullied. I got it because even today, I still don't understand why people don't follow rules. RULES ARE MADE TO BE FOLLOWED, PEOPLE! Did I just yell? Oops, sorry about that. But why can't people follow rules? They are not meant to be broken despite everything you have heard to the contrary. I changed schools, trying to find the best fit. As a teenager, I was a terrible student; I was rude, disruptive, and bored out of my brain. Boarding school was the solution for me. It gave me time away, as I have mentioned previously.

So, back to our boy, now categorised as 2e – twice exceptional.

Seth Perler, a 2e coach, describes 2e as follows:

'Generally speaking, **twice exceptional, or 2e students**, are both intellectually gifted and talented and learning disabled. In the education world, giftedness and learning disabilities are both considered "exceptionalities", so the term "twice-exceptional" refers to a student with exceptionalities on both sides of the proverbial bell curve. In a nutshell, if you have a child who you know is smart/bright, but who struggles to show it, they may be 2e. About 5% of kids are 2e.

On a personal note, I absolutely love working with 2e kids. I often say, "the more complex the kid, the better", because 2e kids are truly the most interesting people I know. They tend to be intellectually deep, incredibly creative, emotionally intense, quirky, and when they get their educational needs met, they do really cool things as adults. Many of the people who "change the world" were 2e kids. They're just super cool

people, and too many of them fall through the cracks because they are misunderstood.'[10]
Seth Perler

Andreas falls under the 2e category because of the hydrocephalus diagnosis. When we first met with Professor Anderson, she seemed surprised when we walked in with Andreas. We now know her surprise was because she had already seen his brain scans, his MRIs, before she met him. His scans show a child who should at least be intellectually disabled, if not physically disabled in some way. But his IQ was compensating for his hydrocephalus. He was presented as 'normal' because of his position on the bell curve. He truly is a wonderful child, made up of all these different elements, which should have stopped him in his tracks. But the universe, the human body, the brain, is a truly remarkable thing.

He watched the world around him and started being a chameleon at a very young age. The teachers at kindergarten and childcare had no idea he could read. They actually discovered it at a special Father's Day night where dads came to visit, and the children showed them around. Andreas was reading a book to Michael in the reading corner and one of the teachers happened to overhear. When Andreas went to play, they questioned Michael. As they hadn't read that book to the class yet, maybe he knew it from home. No, we didn't have it; he was reading and understanding it himself.

So why have I shared this journey with you? I have

already introduced you to our son Anton and the impact his short life had on our family, and how I transitioned into coaching. Well, our first son Andreas is my WHY as well. We all need to have a WHY, and if you don't know what yours is yet, we need to talk!

I could write a book about this amazing human being who is Andreas. I could tell you about his amazing empathy, his sensitivity to others and their emotions, his amazing insights into the human connection, his views on Steven Hawking's work, his desire to become an astrophysicist, his brain surgery, his numerous hospital visits and his academic scholarship to high school … I could go on and on.

But this book is about you and what I want for you. I could talk about Andreas until I am blue in the face. On that, I wonder where that saying came from? Blue in the face. Anyone know? I may have to ask the fount of all knowledge, Google! Okay, I just searched. What did we do before Google? Oh, that's right, we went to the library or had Encyclopedia Britannica or the cheaper version, Funk and Wagnalls (we had the Funk and Wagnalls ones). Oops, sorry got side-tracked a little there. So, back to blue in the face: Google search revealed that it refers to the bluish skin colour resulting from a lack of oxygen, which may result from talking until you run out of breath.

So, what have I learnt from parenting this amazing human being, while working two jobs, and a husband who travels for a living?

I have learnt that everything has happened to me

for a reason. That reason is that I was given an amazing opportunity to take the lessons I had learnt, the mistakes I had made, the resilience I had discovered inside myself, the superpower that I as a mum had, and to share all of this – the good, the bad, the failures, the triumphs – with other mums who found themselves in similar situations.

If I could help just one mum in a room of one hundred people listening to me share my story, then I was selfish not to.

'Your work is going to fill a large part of your life, and the only way to be truly satisfied is to do what you believe is great work. And the only way to do great work is to love what you do. If you haven't found it yet, keep looking. Don't settle. As with all matters of the heart, you'll know when you find it.'

Steve Jobs

CHAPTER 10

Passion Project
The Evolution of the Stress-Free Super Mum

Throughout the book, I have shared my history, my family and my child.

How did I get here, an empowerment coach working with women, mainly mothers, on how they can take back time for themselves?

My business is Stress Free Super Mum; the name is very deliberate.

The first concept I wanted to use was around being a selfish mum because I wanted mums to be selfish for once. But one of my coaches at the time said no to that. He told me that mums wouldn't buy a course showing them how to be selfish.

So, I sat and thought more about what my strengths were. What had I learnt through my life, through those curveballs, that I wanted to share? What was my passion?

My passion was to see every mum living for today, waking up each and every day with a smile on their face and joy in their heart because they were truly living, not just existing. They were choosing themselves and not putting themselves off until the elusive tomorrow, thinking, 'When my children go to school, I will have more time for myself. No, actually, when my children go to high school, um, actually, I'd better wait until my children go to university or college or move out of our home. Then I will have time to paint again or learn how to play a musical instrument or start my business.

That is what I call the land of tomorrow, where all the hopes and dreams that mothers have for themselves hang in a sort of limbo, the pot of gold at the end of the rainbow.

If we, as mothers, stop living in the land of tomorrow and show our children that we matter, that our thoughts and ideas matter, that our self-care matters, that our self-respect matters, we are showing our daughters how to be and showing our sons how to treat women. Yes, you can tell

I am very passionate about this.

In a way, I also decided that I needed to look for the light. I needed to know that my life meant something, that my childhood, my son dying, meant something, that the lessons I learnt weren't to break me. They were to show me that I can thrive through adversity. I can use this to help, to serve, to be that voice on the other end of a phone or via Skype/Zoom. I can be that voice to tell another mother that she is okay, and I will be there to hold her hand and take it one step at a time with her.

I needed not to let life break me. Yes, I throw myself the occasional pity party where I have a pyjamas and Netflix with popcorn day. I'm not Wonder Woman. But it's one day, and the next day I get up and get going. They say that the best way to help yourself is to help others, and I truly believe that. So, who to help?

I was attracted to coaching because, unlike counselling, coaching is all about helping someone move from one point to another. It may be to get away from pain (great motivator) or move to pleasure (not as great a motivator), but it's something the client wants to do. Most of the time, they already have the answers inside themselves. They just need someone to ask the right questions and provide the right amount of accountability for them to see what was right in front of them.

My mentor asked me to find a niche, a niche of potential clients I could help straight away with the knowledge I had then. What knowledge did I have? I listed everything I did and was doing. What stood out the most was parenting this amazing little boy, this child that challenged and amazed me every day. I had already been asked for advice, for help, by other parents. So that is where I started, and my parent-coaching business opened. I hired someone to produce a website for me – more of a virtual business card – to explain who I was, how I worked and why. I was offering my help to mothers parenting neurodiverse children. Neurodiverse refers to the diversity of human minds, the infinite variation in neurocognitive functioning. Winning international awards for this work was truly a humbling experience. The truth about coaching is that coaches aren't successful unless their clients are.

I knew I was meant to be doing what I was doing when I had a client tell me, in one of her first sessions, something she had never told anyone, and that was that she hated her children. She didn't, actually. She was totally and utterly overwhelmed, exhausted and just done. She couldn't see a way forward and was at rock bottom. As a coach, I have no judgement towards my clients. What they tell me is absolutely confidential. I just remember responding with, 'okay, then let's see what we can do to help you with that'. A couple of months later, she rang me in tears and told me that she could now see what others saw in her children and that she loved them. That is why I do what I do.

Another client told me that I saw the greatness in her before she saw it in herself. It reminded me of the following quote from Zig Ziglar:

> 'Surround yourself with the dreamers and the doers, the believers and the thinkers. But most of all, surround yourself with those who see greatness within you, even when you don't see it within yourself.'

That is mainly what coaching is about – having someone walking beside you. Sometimes they may be just in front of you pulling you and at other times behind you giving you a gentle nudge. Or, as one of my clients so elegantly put it, 'I pay you to kick my butt, and it's been the best investment ever.'

Once I had fully established myself as a coach, I found that I was attracting clients who wanted help with structure and organisation. I had been assisting my current clients with this, but their children did not have learning differences or additional needs.

I was being published in magazines and quoted and profiled in others, not only here in Australia but also in the United States, about my thoughts on planning and parenting. I was reaching a wider audience.

Stress-Free Super Mum was born for all mums who want someone who sees them and their potential now, today, not tomorrow. I offered courses mums could do in their own time without me, along with private coaching one-on-one if they needed that extra accountability, that extra push and handholding. I will always offer one-on-one and pro bono coaching, and I will always have a coach myself.

I am one of those coaches who is suspicious of other

coaches that aren't getting coaching themselves. I want to continually improve, learn, be always stepping into the next version of myself, and strive to learn so that I can always bring something new and fresh to my clients. One day, as I set off to attend another seminar, my son mentioned that I was always learning, and I remember responding that a day is wasted if I don't learn anything.

I love seeking out books and references and industry experts so that I can suggest them to my clients to read, research or meet. My clients are my family as well, and I want the very best for them. So, if you are looking for a coach, make sure straight away that you feel they are there for you and with you.

I have held seminars, given workshops and spoken on stage to just a few people or an entire auditorium. To share my message of mothers having the space and grace for themselves is an absolute privilege.

This is my legacy. This is my footprint – to leave hope and joy in the hearts of the mothers I work with.

What I want for you is for you to find your legacy, your joy, because when you do, the ripple effect of all of us doing that will change the world.

'Imagine a world where everyone lived their passion.'
– Jay Shetty

Imagine it, and it all starts with YOU.

Live with passion, intention and purpose!

Remember always. You are the most important person in your life.

Xxx Katrina

Katrina is sharing more in her INTERACTIVE book.

See exclusive videos, audios and photos.

DOWNLOAD it now at www.deanpublishing.com/warrior

CHAPTER 11

Summary of Tools, Techniques and Quotes from Each Chapter

Chapter One: Wear Your Warrior

'I choose
To live by choice, not by chance,
To be motivated, not manipulated,
To be useful, not used,
To make changes, not excuses,
To excel, not compete.
I choose self-esteem, not self-pity,
I choose to listen to my inner voice, not to the random opinions of others.
I choose to do the things that you won't so I can continue to do the things you can't.'
Dr Bohdi Sanders

Chapter Two: Self Love Selfish or Selfless?

'You are the longest commitment you'll ever have. You have to make you a priority.'
Anon

'Today you are You, that is truer than true. There is no one alive who is Youer than You.'
Dr Suess

'You must take personal responsibility. You cannot change the circumstances, the seasons, or the wind, but you can change yourself.'
Jim Rohn

Affirmations

I am Brave.

I am Kind.

I am Smart.

I am Strong.

I am Helpful.

I am Beautiful.

SUMMARY OF TOOLS, TECHNIQUES AND QUOTES FROM EACH CHAPTER

I can do Hard Things.

I am Grateful.

I am Loved.

I am Enough.

Chapter Three: Control

*'God grant me the serenity
to accept the things I cannot change,
courage to change the things I can,
and wisdom to know the difference.'*
Reinhold Niebuhr

Overwhelm exercise using post-it notes
Two groups:

Circle of Influence –
have control over

Circle of Concern –
no control over

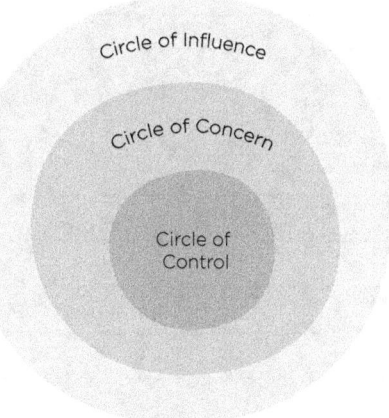

Worksheet

Today

Tomorrow

Next Week

Chapter Four: Buy Back Your Time

'Time Management is really a misnomer — the challenge is not to manage time, but to manage ourselves. The key is not to prioritise what's on your schedule, but to schedule your priorities.'
Stephen Covey

Time Calculation sheet with 30-minute intervals
Example categories

- Work
- Household cleaning
- Grocery shopping
- Time with children
- Time with partner
- Netflix/Foxtel/Stan, etc.
- Facebook/Pinterest/Instagram/Social Media
- Time just for me (self-care)
- Exercise
- Food preparation
- Family time

Urgent/Important Matrix

	Urgent	Not Urgent
Important	**DO NOW** (Urgent | Important)	**DO LATER** (Not Urgent | Important)
Not Important	**DELEGATE** (Urgent | Not Important)	**DITCH** (Not Urgent | Not Important)

Age-Appropriate jobs/chores for children
Ages 2-3

- Pick up toys
- Wipe up spills
- Dust
- Clear away their plate/cup at mealtimes
- Help unpack and put away groceries

- Sort recycling
- Put dirty clothes in their clothes basket

Ages 4-6

- All chores from the ages 2-3 category
- Make their bed
- Sort laundry and put away clothes
- Feed pets
- Make a snack
- Set the table and clear it
- Help in the garden - water plants and weed

Ages 7-9

- All chores from the previous two categories
- Get themselves up in the morning with an alarm clock
- Make their own school lunch
- Manage their pocket money
- Fold their own laundry
- Cook simple food
- Load and unload the dishwasher
- Vacuum

Ages 10+
- All chores from the previous three categories
- Use the washing machine and dryer
- Mow the lawns
- Basic home repairs
- Family budgeting (help to budget for school trips and family holidays)
- Find paid jobs for neighbours (bringing in their rubbish bins, feeding and walking animals, etc.)
- Cook a complete meal
- Wash the car

Chapter Five: Planning

'It takes as much energy to wish as it does to plan.'
Eleanor Roosevelt

Chore Charts

Meal Planning

Meal Prepping

Sunday Set-up: Plan, Prepare and Organise

SUMMARY OF TOOLS, TECHNIQUES AND QUOTES FROM EACH CHAPTER

Chapter Six: Your Dream Day

'The biggest adventure you can take is to live the life of your dreams.'
Oprah Winfrey

Scheduling your Calendar

Morning and Evening Routines

Morning Routine
Mind
-
-
-
-
-

Body
-
-
-
-
-

Goals
-
-
-
-
-

Nutrition
-
-
-
-
-

Chapter Seven: Have you Kondoed?

'The best way to find out what we really need is to get rid of what we don't.'
Marie Kondo

Decluttering Scenarios: Swedish Death Cleaning, Selling Your Home, Transferring Overseas, Mother-in-law visiting.

'A dream written down with a date becomes a goal. A goal broken down into steps becomes a plan. A plan backed by action makes your dreams come true.'
Greg S. Reid

Chapter Eight: Law of Attraction

'Whether you think you can or think you can't, either way you are right.'
Henry Ford

Vision Boards

The Twelve Universal Laws
1. **Law of Divine Oneness** – this is that we are all

connected. So, what we think, say and do will have an effect on others and the universe around us.

2. **Law of Vibration** – everything in the universe moves and vibrates. The same principles of vibrating in the physical world also apply to our thoughts and feelings. Each sound, object and thought has its own vibrational frequency.

3. **Law of Action** – I think you all know how I feel about this one. We must engage in actions that support our thoughts, dreams, goals, emotions and words.

4. **Law of Correspondence** – this is related to the Law of Divine Oneness. Throughout the universe, there are repetitive patterns. Significant patterns can repeat on smaller scales.

5. **Law of Cause and Effect** – nothing happens by chance or outside of these laws. Every action has a reaction or consequence.

6. **Law of Compensation** – the old adage of you reap what you sow. What you put out into the world will correspond with what you receive from the world.

7. **Law of Attraction** – in brief, we create the things, events and people that come into our lives. Our

thoughts, feelings, words and actions produce energies, which in turn attract like energies.

8. **Law of Perpetual Transmutation of Energy** – now that's a mouthful. This means that everything around us is in a constant state of flux, and higher vibrations can affect lower vibrations. The best way to understand this one is when you are feeling low, being around someone who is happy and encouraging to you can lift you up, therefore changing your vibration.

9. **Law of Relativity** – there is a saying that if you are with a group of friends and you all put your problems in a basket, and everyone got to choose which problem they would take out, everyone would take their own back. This law is about comparing our problems to others with a proper and clear perspective. No matter how bad we perceive our situation to be, there is always someone worse off; it's all relative.

10. **Law of Polarity** – everything has an opposite. The existence of opposites help us understand our lives and help us be resilient in hard times – the old silver lining adage.

11. **Law of Rhythm** – linked to the Law of Vibration but opens it up more, in that not only does everything move and vibrate, but everything also has cycles as

well. Think of the seasons, the body's aging process, a season for everything and everything has a season.

12. **Law of Gender** – no, not talking about whether you are a female or male. This is about the fact that there are two types of energy, masculine energy and feminine energy, and we all possess some amount of each. It's finding the balance between the two. (https://www.thelawofattraction.com)

Chapter Nine: Motherhood

'Here's to the crazy ones. The misfits. The rebels. The troublemakers. The round pegs in the square holes. The ones who see things differently. They're not fond of rules. And they have no respect for the status quo. You can quote them, disagree with them, glorify or vilify them. About the only thing you can't do is ignore them. Because they change things. They push the human race forward. And while some may see them as the crazy ones, we see genius. Because the people who are crazy enough to think they can change the world are the ones who do'.
Rob Siltanen

Parenting Styles

- Authoritarian or Disciplinarian
- Permissive or Indulgent
- Uninvolved
- Authoritative

Chapter Ten: Passion Project

'Your work is going to fill a large part of your life, and the only way to be truly satisfied is to do what you believe is great work. And the only way to do great work is to love what you do. If you haven't found it yet, keep looking. Don't settle. As with all matters of the heart, you'll know when you find it.'
Steve Jobs

'Surround yourself with the dreamers and the doers, the believers and the thinkers. But most of all surround yourself with those who see greatness within you, even when you don't see it within yourself.'
Zig Ziglar

'Imagine a world where everyone lived their passion.'
Jay Shetty

NOTES

NOTES

KATRINA WURM

NOTES

KATRINA WURM

Testimonials/Case Studies/ Working with Clients

I was feeling overwhelmed, challenged by motherhood and my teenage children. I had lost my confidence and felt hopeless and exhausted.

I saw Katrina's Facebook post on becoming a life coach. I wanted to do something to help me be a better person, a better mum. I realised that I needed assistance and after speaking with Katrina, knew she and I were a great match.

In my coaching sessions Katrina provided me with a safe and comfortable environment where I am able to let down my guard and speak my truth from the heart without judgement.

I honestly feel that I have Katrina in my corner, supporting me with my successes and holding my hand through challenges. Katrina has successfully helped me navigate through the peaks and troughs that life has handed me. She has helped me to use these moments to help teach both myself and my children how to handle adversity and build resilience.

This process wasn't easy; at times it was confronting, it bought up emotions I had suppressed for many years. It was life changing, though. Throughout my coaching, Katrina has held me accountable for my actions and behaviours and made me face up to my fears, helping me to believe in myself and my dreams and made me truly believe that I am worth it!

Katrina actively listens with empathy and compassion. One of the most significant things I have learnt from Katrina is that I need to continually challenge my beliefs. I now understand the things I resist in life will persist. I need to approach situations with openness and curiosity, to gain a greater understanding before taking action.

My coaching sessions honestly are something that I look forward to each week. I face each day with the knowledge that I have Katrina there supporting me and helping me to be the best version of myself that I can be.

With the coaching I have received from Katrina, I have clarity, I have strength, I am confident and I have the will to make the most of this life I live.

I would definitely recommend Katrina Wurm to help you navigate the challenges of your life and to help you be the best possible version of yourself that you can be.

D.C.
Manager
Mother to four children

Katrina has become my reliable sounding board. Each week she offers new insights and tools to improve my daily patterns and behaviours as I work toward my version of a better me. Throughout my coaching experience, Katrina was able to quickly identify the wood from the trees and make each 45-minute session both productive and satisfying. She is a supportive listener and a champion of my goals. Ultimately, I enjoyed Katrina's honest approach, which gave me confidence in both her professionalism and my ability to achieve the outcomes I was aiming for. Thank you, Katrina. I look forward to working with you further.

D.A.
Trainer/Facilitator
Mother to two children

I was in a very dark grey unrelenting world. Where everything seemed to be caving in on me, and I knew I needed to change something. I decided it was time and I made the life changing decision to make changes in my life, and I signed up for life coaching with Katrina. I knew it was going to require hard work, that I'd face many challenges and that I had to look really deeply at myself and be ready to face some deep demons. Katrina was my steady hand, she held me accountable for many decisions, questioned my every move, gently guiding and challenging me. My world began to have light once more. I thank Katrina so much for helping, guiding, protecting and challenging me. My life now has so much light that I decided to continue for another six months.

Thank you very much Katrina, and I am looking forward to challenging my world.

E.G.
High school teacher
Mother to four children

Taking on a life coach was not something I had planned. However, it is a decision that could possibly prove to be one of the most crucial turning points in my adult life, acting as a catalyst that, over mere months, has produced several forks on my professional road, and I can see more coming in my future. Having Katrina in my corner holding me accountable, spurring me on, offering suggestions, picking me up on negative self-talk, resulted in me achieving my goal before my first month of meeting with her was even over. So, we moved on to a new goal! Each week I felt a strong but not overwhelming push to do my best work for her – what would I tell Katrina this week in terms of achievements? Had I done what I had set out to do in our last meeting? She did not wave a magic wand to make me achieve my smaller aims on the way to my larger goal but made me believe that I could achieve these things on my own, and so I did. I recommend Katrina as a supportive, positive but unrelenting companion on whichever journey you choose to travel and whatever goal you choose to pursue.

J.D.
Head of a non-profit
Mother to two children

I had often heard about 'coaching' in the corporate world and never really thought a life coach would be of any value to me. I was so wrong. Curiosity got the better of me when I read about Katrina and her life coaching business.

From my first point of contact Katrina was the epitome of professionalism.

Through our one-on-one sessions, Katrina enabled me to recognise, set and prioritise my goals.

The sessions provided lots of positive reinforcement and a framework to help me identify the changes I wanted to make. I was set up for success … without even realising it! I achieved my first goal much sooner than I even thought possible.

Katrina always had my back and always knew the right questions to ask, enabling me to be successful. I really looked forward to telling Katrina of my achievements each week. Even if I didn't feel I had achieved anything, Katrina was always able to highlight and remind me of my successes relative to my goals.

The skills I have learnt I know I will be able to call on in any life situation.

Thank you, Katrina … you make a difference!

J.W.
Medical field
Mother to two children

Over the past few months, I have been receiving coaching from Katrina to help me work on a goal I have had ever since I can remember – to write and publish a novel. I was plodding along slowly on my own but with Katrina's help I managed to write 50,000 words in two months, finish off my novel and begin editing. I also have a plan to get my name out in the writing community so that I can publish my novel within the year.

In my sessions with Katrina, she kept me focused on my goal and helped me work through any challenges I was facing. I felt that she was genuinely invested in my goal as much as I was, and the outcome was priceless. I managed to reach my lifelong goal of writing a novel. Despite Katrina not being familiar with the workings of the writing and publishing world, she always had suggestions and questions to help me move forward.

I would thoroughly recommend Katrina as a coach if you have a goal you want to work towards. I looked forward to our sessions where I shared my wins and challenges for the week and worked out what was next. I already thought life was pretty good but after working with Katrina, I am genuinely the happiest I have ever been. I am doing what I love and a step closer to publishing my book. I can't thank you enough Katrina!

K.B.
Entrepreneur
Mother to three children

I reflect on my time with Katrina as one of the most positive experiences I have had over recent years. I have friends who have mentioned their life coaches but had no idea what this was all about. I was presented with an opportunity to work with Katrina and although I wasn't sure what to expect I felt completely comfortable with her approach and honesty.

I was feeling frustrated about the lack of clarity I had with my future path, personal and professional. I had ideas and goals, but I wasn't able to see a way to make them come to fruition, sometimes I just couldn't see the wood for the trees.

Working with Katrina has been challenging and extremely rewarding. Katrina is very passionate about her vocation as a life coach. I have been stretched and challenged like never before. Katrina has only MY wellbeing, potential and joy of life at the forefront of her coaching approach, and I value her support. Katrina provided me with ideas, affirmations and strategies that have made my ideas and goals realistic and doable.

The coaching sessions lasted around 45 minutes. In the first session, Katrina covered what to expect from her and what she expects from me. I've never experienced a conversation with someone who only has my vested interest at heart. We got to know each other and understand the process. Katrina would start each session asking what wins I had experienced during the week and how I felt about them and also what I had experienced that was not such a win and how I responded to that. I was set tasks/homework to challenge myself to push me out of my comfort zone and strategies to change my attitude about myself and life in general, not always easy but it did get easier with Katrina's positive reinforcement.

I now feel more confident because I have some great tools that Katrina has given me to realise my potential and listen to my own heart and desires to achieve what I want to do, and to invest my time in positive lifestyles. I feel more confident in my convictions and know that I too have a voice that deserves to be heard. These tools I will always be truly grateful for. This is my experience with Katrina, and I can highly recommend her as a life coach.

R.E.
Administrator
Mother to two children

Appendix 1

Welcome To Holland

by Emily Perl Kingsley
Copyright©1987 by Emily Perl Kingsley.
All rights reserved.
Reprinted by permission of the author.

I am often asked to describe the experience of raising a child with a disability – to try to help people who have not shared that unique experience to understand it, to imagine how it would feel. It's like this……

When you're going to have a baby, it's like planning a fabulous vacation trip – to Italy. You buy a bunch of guide books and make your wonderful plans. The Coliseum. The Michelangelo David. The gondolas in Venice. You may learn some handy phrases in Italian. It's all very exciting.

After months of eager anticipation, the day finally arrives. You pack your bags and off you go. Several hours later, the plane lands. The flight attendant comes in and says, "Welcome to Holland."

"Holland?!?" you say. "What do you mean Holland?? I signed up for Italy! I'm supposed to be in Italy. All my life I've dreamed of going to Italy."

But there's been a change in the flight plan. They've landed in Holland and there you must stay.

The important thing is that they haven't taken you to a

horrible, disgusting, filthy place, full of pestilence, famine and disease. It's just a different place.

So you must go out and buy new guide books. And you must learn a whole new language. And you will meet a whole new group of people you would never have met.

It's just a different place. It's slower-paced than Italy, less flashy than Italy. But after you've been there for a while and you catch your breath, you look around …. and you begin to notice that Holland has windmills …. and Holland has tulips. Holland even has Rembrandts.

But everyone you know is busy coming and going from Italy … and they're all bragging about what a wonderful time they had there. And for the rest of your life, you will say "Yes, that's where I was supposed to go. That's what I had planned."

And the pain of that will never, ever, ever, ever go away … because the loss of that dream is a very very significant loss.

But … if you spend your life mourning the fact that you didn't get to Italy, you may never be free to enjoy the very special, the very lovely things … about Holland.

Appendix 2

'The Road not Taken' by Robert Frost (1916)

Two roads diverged in a yellow wood,
And sorry I could not travel both
And be one traveler, long I stood
And looked down one as far as I could
To where it bent in the undergrowth;

Then took the other, as just as fair,
And having perhaps the better claim,
Because it was grassy and wanted wear;
Though as for that the passing there
Had worn them really about the same,

And both that morning equally lay
In leaves no step had trodden black.
Oh, I kept the first for another day!
Yet knowing how way leads on to way,
I doubted if I should ever come back.

I shall be telling this with a sigh
Somewhere ages and ages hence:
Two roads diverged in a wood, and I
I took the one less traveled by,
And that has made all the difference.

Appendix 3

Reflective Questions

For You to ask Yourself

1. What are you excited about right now?

2. What was your first thought when you woke up today?

3. What do you want to accomplish by your next birthday?

4. If you could be famous for one thing, what would it be?

5. What's the best thing about your life?

6. What's a small thing that makes you feel happy?

7. What's something you want to do, but you can't yet?

8. What makes you feel loved?

9. What will you be doing in 10 years?

10. If you could only eat one food for an entire year, what would you choose?

11. If you could have one superpower, what would it be?

12. What's the best thing that has ever happened to you?

13. What's the worst thing that has ever happened to you?

14. What are you most proud of?

15. Which rule do you have to follow that doesn't make sense?

16. If you could pack anything in your lunch tomorrow, what would it be?

17. What makes you feel special?

18. If you had to choose only three words to describe yourself, what would you say?

19. If you were invisible, where would you go and what would you do?

20. What do you worry about the most?

21. What's something you're looking forward to?

22. When do you feel happiest?

23. What's the most important thing you've learnt so far?

24. What's your favourite joke?

25. What is one thing you want to learn how to do?

26. If you could stay up all night, what would you do?

For You to ask Your Family

1. What's your favourite thing to do as a family?

2. What's something nice someone said to you lately?

3. Who understands you the best?

4. If you could change one family rule, what would it be?

5. What's your favourite thing to do with your friends?

6. If you could switch places with one person for a day, who would it be?

7. What's something you did to help someone today?

8. What do you get to do at someone else's house that you wish you could do at ours?

9. What advice would you give to a younger sister or brother?

10. What's the smartest thing you heard somebody say today?

11. Who made you smile today?

12. What's your favourite family tradition? Why?

13. What's the funniest thing somebody did or said today?

14. What was the last time someone was mad at you?

15. If we didn't have to go to school or work on Monday, what would you want to do all day?

16. Has someone ever asked you to do something you didn't want to do?

17. What's the most important thing for a parent to do?

18. Twenty years from now, where do you think you'll live?

19. What's the biggest problem in our world?

20. If you could give everybody in the world one piece of advice, what would it be?

21. If you could create one law that everybody on earth had to follow, what would it be?

22. If you could learn any language, what would you learn?

23. What will the world be like in ten years? What will be the same? What will be different?

24. If you could live in another country for one year, where would you live?

Katrina is sharing more in her INTERACTIVE book.

See exclusive videos, audios and photos.

DOWNLOAD it now at www.deanpublishing.com/warrior

About the Author

Katrina Wurm is an empowerment coach who specialises in assisting women to lead their best lives. She arms her clients with a range of tools and strategies to help them prioritise self-care and grant them the freedom to pursue their true purpose.

She is the proud recipient of international awards for her coaching and has been quoted and profiled in many different publications and news articles worldwide.

INTRODUCING KATRINA

For most of us, living our dream life seems to be a notion doomed to float amongst the stars. Too often, we are held back by what we think we should be doing and what we feel is safe. Katrina Wurm has experienced many challenges and much adversity throughout her life. Against the odds and through sheer determination, she has been able to make the

impossible possible. By learning from, rather than being beaten by, obstacles, Katrina has been able to navigate her life's path to her dream life. Now an empowerment coach, she enjoys helping others traverse hardships to those she experienced herself. Katrina gives her clients the guidance and tools they need to empower themselves to live their best life.

Born to learn

From a young age, Katrina showed great focus and direction. She always excelled academically and was successful in her school and university life. Katrina entered into a double degree and was accepted into the Royal Military College at Duntroon. This was no mean feat. However, it didn't take her long to realise that she was doing the course for someone else, not herself. Sometimes even the most driven people can be driving down the wrong road. Katrina had the courage to realise this about herself and forged forward. She began another degree that steered her in the direction she felt more aligned with, management, training and development. This was a taste of her future aspirations.

Selfish or self-care?

The main lesson Katrina took from her early years was

that no matter what adversity she was facing in her life, she needed to take the time to look after herself. It was not a simple transition and remains something she works on to this day. But she can identify her value and makes time to be kind and care for herself. The majority of us, particularly parents, can identify with this internal war between the feeling of selfishness or guilt of caring for ourselves instead of self-care. This is one of the first steps Katrina helps her clients take in creating their best life and making the impossible possible. How can you live your best life if you don't value the person who is living it?

Taking control

The other challenge Katrina undertook on her journey towards achieving her dream was taking control and learning to relinquish it. As a coach, Katrina educates her clients on how to take control of their lives by always using time to their advantage – by scheduling, mapping out and planning. But as we all know, there are some things in life that we cannot control. Katrina felt this acutely over an agonising 12 years of trying to become pregnant. After many miscarriages, Katrina finally gave birth to a beautiful boy. She persisted in trying to expand her family, and a further pregnancy with triplets ended in one live birth and that baby passing away within the day. Heartbreak after heartbreak left Katrina worn down and feeling as though she had never entirely been in control of her body for all those years.

After all this heartache, she discovered her first son had several physical complications requiring such ordeals as brain surgery, amongst others, a diagnosis of 2e, or twice-exceptional. Katrina likens her parent journey to taking a trip to Paris when you thought you were headed to Rome. Of course, it's different from what you expected, but you will find beauty in either country when it comes down to it. As you can imagine, after reading about her tumultuous and brave journey, all these difficulties have shaped her as a person, mother, friend, worker and wife. This life-changing lesson in control of what she could and could not affect enabled Katrina to regain control of her life.

Living the impossible dream – your best life

All these events led Katrina to where she is today. She trained under the best life coach in Australia. She learnt to implement her tools from her learnings and that of her coach to help others live their best life. In doing so, Katrina came to realise she had made her own impossible possible – her life as a coach *was* her dream life. Who could be more perfect for holding your hand on your own journey than someone who has lived it all and arrived at the destination?

Katrina is able to use her life experiences to assist and coach other parents who have gifted children or children with additional needs and any Mum who feels overwhelmed with their daily life. She believes that everyone is put on this earth for a reason. Hers is to steer others in the direction of

ABOUT THE AUTHOR

making their impossible possible.

Katrina says, 'Never let what happens to you define you. Choose how to define yourself.' This is the heart of her story and success. Too many of us hide our true aspirations due to fear: fear of failing, fear of being unsafe, insecure, appearing wrong, or many other reasons. Though it took Katrina a roundabout way, her path led her to where she is today – a life coach with a flexible schedule to be available to her family. She has a fulfilling job where she is able to empower others to live their best lives, and by doing so, she is living hers.

www.stressfreesupermum.com
www.katrinawurm.com.au
www.facebook.com/KatrinaWurmEmpowermentCoaching/

Katrina's Product Range
www.stressfreesupermum.com/shop

Acknowledgements

Writing a book, especially one that shares your own life, own experiences and innermost thoughts is not only cathartic but as scary as hell.

I grew up with parents who, in their own way, loved me and showed me that love, empathy and compassion are what makes the world go around.

To my sister, my best friend – life would be empty without you.

To my kind, compassionate brother – you are truly amazing and a wonderful father.

I would not be here today, sitting writing this, living my passion coaching other women on their own journey without my own coaches and mentors. Scott Harris, Chris and Harriet Duncan – thank you for your coaching and support. To Sam Cawthorn, you gave me the courage to 'speak' my story. And to one of the most fabulous women I know – Susan Dean – you gave me the final push to share my story with words through this book. Your family, your staff, Nat – you would have to be the best editor in the world – you people truly are the only ones I would trust

ACKNOWLEDGEMENTS

with this, my life bared to the world.

My ladies, the ones I share my life with, my childhood friends who have been there for every step of my journey, have held me as I cried, who laughed with me so that my stomach hurt the next day, we have known each other for 35+ years and life is so full of light because I have all of you.

My clients who have welcomed me into their lives, I will forever take it as an honour for you to share your lives with me. You are my greatest inspiration and I will continue to strive to be better each day, so that I can continue to serve all of you, with all of me.

Andreas – my boy, you challenge, amaze and delight me every day. You are the reason I am the mother I am, and the lessons we learn together are the reason I support the women who come to me for advice. I love watching as you grow and know you will change the world.

My Anton – my baby boy, you started all of this! You were only with us for a short period of time, but your impact has been felt worldwide, and I do what I do in honour of you.

To my husband, Michael, who said yes, yes to me embarking on this journey of becoming a Coach and an international multiple award-winning one at that! (still humbled by that), you have supported me, and given me free rein to do what lights me up. You have shown me what a man, husband and father truly is: strong, courageous with every decision you make underpinned by love for your family. I am forever grateful you chose me to share your life with. I thank you and love you, always.

To everyone who is reading this book, remember each day you are amazing, you deserve love, respect, empathy and compassion and YOU MATTER!

Live with Passion, Intention and Purpose!
Katrina

ENDNOTES

1. Merriam-Webster. (n.d.). Warrior. In *Merriam-Webster.com dictionary*. Retrieved August 15, 2021, from https://www.merriam-webster.com/dictionary/warrior

2. Cambridge Dictionary. (n.d.). Warrior. In *Cambridge Dictionary*. Retrieved August 15, 2021, from https://dictionary.cambridge.org/dictionary/english/warrior

3. Campbell, J 1990, *The Hero's Journey: Joseph Campbell on His Life and Work*, HarperCollins, New York City.

4. Freeman, C 2016, *The Power of Done: Effective Strategies for Coaches, Consultants, and C-Level Execs*, Dynamic Life, California.

5. Sanders, B 2011, *Modern Bushido: Living a Life of Excellence*, Kaizen Quest Publishing, Colorado.

6. Covey, S 1989, *The 7 Habits of Highly Effective People*, Free Press, New York.

7. Baumrind, D 1991, 'Parenting styles and adolescent development', in J Brooks-Gunn, RM Lerner & AC Petersen (eds.), *The Encyclopaedia on Adolescence*, Garland Publishing, New York, pp. 746-748.

8. Better Health Channel (n.d.), Slow transit constipation, accessed 30 April 2021, https://www.betterhealth.vic.gov.au/health/ConditionsAndTreatments/slow-transit-constipation

    Andrews, CN & Storr, M 2011, 'The pathology of chronic constipation', *Canadian Journal of Gastroenterology= Journal canadien de gastroenterologie*, 25 Suppl B(Suppl B), 16B–21B.

9. Better Health Channel (n.d.), Hydrocephalus, accessed 30 April 2021, https://www.betterhealth.vic.gov.au/health/ConditionsAndTreatments/hydrocephalus

10. Perler, S (n.d.), Is my child twice exceptional or 2e? [The Ultimate Guide], https://sethperler.com/child-2e-twice-exceptional-ultimate-guide/

PERMISSIONS

Appendix 1 - Kingsley, Emily Perl. Poem – 'Welcome To Holland', Copyright©1987 by Emily Perl Kingsley. All rights reserved. Reprinted by permission of the author.

Appendix 2 - Frost, Robert (1916) 'The Road Not Taken', Public domain.

Seth Perler for permission to use his article 'Is my Child Twice Exceptional or 2e? [The Ultimate Guide]' and his insights and wisdom.
https://sethperler.com

www.ingramcontent.com/pod-product-compliance
Lightning Source LLC
Chambersburg PA
CBHW071614080526
44588CB00010B/1123